Shrinking
the *Judge*
Freeing the *Inner Child*

Rick Malter, Ph.D.
Rosalie Malter, M.A.

Malter Institute for Natural Development, Inc.
2500 West Higgins Road, Suite 355
Hoffman Estates, IL 60195
(847) 519-0220   Fax: (847) 519-9732
(800) 882-3015

2nd printing January 1998 USA

Printed and bound in the United States of America
ISBN: 0-87418-322-7

Table of Contents

Chapter 1: What is the *Judge* 1

Chapter 2: How the *Judge* Develops in Childhood 29

Chapter 3: The *Judge* in Dysfunctional Families 53

Chapter 4: The Mind-Body Connection: Another
    View of the *Judge* 67

Chapter 5: Jungian Archetypes and the *Judge* 81

Chapter 6: The *Judge* and Psychotherapy 93

Chapter 7:   The *Judge* in Recovery:
    Addictions and Codependence 125

Chapter 8: The *Judge* and Sexuality 143

Chapter 9: The *Judge* in Health Care 163

Chapter 10: The *Judge* in Individual and Social Change 187

References and Suggested Readings

KEY CONCEPTS RELATED
TO THE *JUDGE*

1. The *Judge* incorporates verbal messages, visual images and memories, and the body's stress reaction into a powerful personality matrix buried deep within the human psyche.

2. The development of the *Judge* and its incorporation into human personality are inherent to human nature and the way in which our body and mind are connected by the basic stress resonse — the fight or flight response.

3. We now have therapeutic techniques which help us to shrink the *Judge* and greatly reduce its destructive psychological effect on our lives, but we can never eliminate the *Judge* completely.

4. Our perception of the *Judge* and our reactions to it are very personal and subjective. Our own *Judge* is unique to each of us.

5. The *Judge* is within us psychologically and it is also all around us — in our relationships, families, schools, jobs, and society.

6. The concept of the *Judge* helps us to better account for some of the paradoxes of life — why making important positive life changes may trigger intense anxiety and depression for some people.

7. The concept of the *Judge* helps us to better understand perfectionism and its destructive effect on people's lives.

Rick Malter, Ph.D. & Rosalie Malter, M.A.
Malter Institute for Natural Development
2500 W. Higgins Road, Suite 355
Hoffman Estates, IL 60195
(847) 519-0220   Fax: (847) 519-9732
(800) 882-3015
rickmind@aol.com

Acknowledgments

We are grateful to our mentor, Dr. John Cooper, and to his colleagues — Tassia Riordan and Rebecca Pillsbury — who first taught us about the *Judge* and its destructive role in people's lives and in society. We are also grateful to our friends and colleagues, Ann Scanlan, Renee Nataro and Ed McHugh, and to our many clients who have taught us so much more about the *Judge* and how to deflate its power over people's lives. Although the client stories in this book are composites, we thank all of the clients whose courage and openness in individual therapy, groups, and workshops gave us the stories, drawings, and clay sculpts on which to build this work.

We wish to thank our editor, Virginia McCullough, whose grasp of this material and how it should be communicated was invaluable in bringing this work to print. We also are indebted to her friend, Julia Schopick, for creating such a wonderful match with Virginia. Barbara and Bob Roehrich were very supportive in encouraging us to undertake this project. They were highly instrumental in getting this project off the ground.

We wish to thank our children and their spouses who were all very patient and tolerant of the time and effort it took for us to write and complete this book. We thank them for their helpful advice about marketing, graphics, and computers related to the completion of this book. We also wish to thank Kym Beckman, Max Brand, and Anna Jaffe for their illustrations that have added so much to the book.

We dedicate this book to our grandchildren, Ariella, Danny, Ma'ayan, and Meirav, and to those yet unborn, with hopes that they will grow up more *Judge*-free than we did. We hope that they will live in a more *Judge*-free world than we have experienced.

Rick and Rosalie Malter

Author's Note

Although this book describes some psychologically and emotionally intense situations related to the *Judge*, the book's purpose is for educating and informing people about this profoundly important psychological concept. The book should not in any way be used to diagnose psychiatric, psychological and emotional problems. If you need help with such problems, seek the services of a qualified professional to make a diagnosis and to offer appropriate treatment.

For some people, the material in this book may stir up strong emotional reactions, most likely related to their own *Judge*. Since the *Judge* is triggered by stress and tension, being able to deep breathe, stretch and relax can often help to reduce the intensity of such emotional reactions. Refer to Chapter 4 for some suggestions and guidelines.

Introduction

This book allows us to share with you what we have been privileged to learn and experience in our psychotherapy work, using a profound psychological concept that we refer to as the *Judge*. We believe that this concept, unique in its simplicity, is very powerful psychologically in facilitating healing, recovery and fundamental life changes. You will have the opportunity to read about our clients' experiences in psychotherapy and in our weekend intensive workshops on the *Judge* and the *inner child*. The results of their courage and willingness to confront and defuse the power of the *Judge* over their lives give all of us hope and encouragement that meaningful psychological change is possible for many people. This work empowers a person to really take charge of living his or her life to its fullest potential.

We believe in an integrated approach to treatment, one that uses the wisdom of many fields, including psychology, addiction and recovery programs and the ancient philosophies of spiritual growth. Chapter by chapter, you will learn about the many ways in which the *Judge* has affected your life and the lives of those around you. Of equal or even greater importance, you will learn how the psychological power of the *Judge* can be defused and diminished, allowing you to experience a greater flow of love and life energies.

Many readers will wonder what makes the *Judge* so different from other similar types of psychological concepts — Freud's *superego,* Transactional Analysis' *Critical Parent,* the *Inner Critic,* etc. Our experience, both personally and professionally, is that the *Judge* can be made concrete and tangible so that it can be seen and felt by a person during the therapy process. There are also some psychologically important, but very subtle aspects to the way in which the *Judge* operates in an individual's personality that need to be taken into account. There is also a strong connection between the *Judge* and stress. As long as the *Judge* is active in a personality, but outside conscious awareness, high stress levels can be triggered for no apparent reason. As we will explain later in this book, when the psychological power of the *Judge* is defused in the therapeutic process, people experience a great sense of relief from tension and a substantial drop in their internal stress.

We will also show you later in the book how the concept of the *Judge* can be meaningfully related to the concept of the *inner child* and to the Jungian concept of the *Warrior* archetype. This relationship forms a highly effective psychological model that can be used to empower a person's emotional healing and recovery. We will show you a graphic illustration of this model and how we view the three parts in relationship to each other. The illustration will help you to see how the *Judge* dominates the *inner child*. It is exactly this view of the *Judge* dominating the *inner child* that makes clear why some approaches to doing only *inner child* therapy work can be psychologically hazardous for some people.

We believe that just about everyone can benefit from the exploration of the *Judge* concept that we offer here. It would be a rare person, indeed, who has not suffered psychologically in some way because of the *Judge*. People with chronic depression, obsessive compulsive disorder (OCD) or those who experience panic attacks, low self-esteem, lack of self-confidence or have a history of troubled professional or personal relationships and so on, can all benefit from exploring the *Judge* concept.

Because of the recent interest in the emotional and spiritual issues involved in addictions and recovery, we have found that our recovering clients can comprehend and apply the *Judge* concept. They use this concept as a particularly powerful tool to heal the emotional wounds that are so strongly related to addictions, codependency, abuse and dysfunctional family relationships.

In general, doing *"Judge*-work" can benefit just about anyone who wants to continue to grow emotionally and spiritually, no matter whether the person has significant psychological difficulties or previous treatment. You don't have to be "crazy" or "mentally ill" to derive a great deal of benefit from working on your *Judge*, because, psychologically, the *Judge* is inherently a part of the human condition. Each of us carries a *Judge* in our psyche. For some of us, the *Judge* is dormant and doesn't affect us to any great extent. It lies deep within our psyche and is psychologically encapsulated. It takes an intense stressor to break through this encapsulation to trigger a response from the *Judge*. For others, though, the *Judge* totally dominates their lives. They are flooded with self-doubt and anxiety. They can become immobilized with deep depression and feelings of worthlessness. It is a struggle for them just to get through every single day.

We believe that the *Judge* concept is a major part of the recent development in practical psychological ideas that have helped many individuals, both within and outside the mental health and psychotherapy fields. We have been psychotherapists for more than 25 years and no single concept has had more profound implications for us both personally and professionally than the *Judge* concept. We are also educators and believe strongly in communicating concepts and ideas that can help people to gain a greater understanding of themselves. The concept of the *Judge* — its origins in childhood and its effects on adults — can be empowering for you, too. Nevertheless, the *Judge* can be a very destructive force when it operates within each of us, but outside our conscious awareness. However, when it is confronted and unmasked, its destructive power over our lives is greatly diminished. With greater awareness and understanding, you can keep it from regaining power and control over your life.

The concept of the *Judge* helps us to understand that, despite all of our technological and cultural advances, there still remains within each of us a powerfully destructive psychological force. What we call the *Judge* is this destructive force. One of the most important things you will learn from this book is that it is our own anger and fear that give the *Judge* energy and power to dominate us. We need to learn to recognize this fact and to take greater personal responsibility for our own anger and fear. This is a crucial point that we will explain in greater detail later in the book. The *Judge* really has no power or energy of its own. It becomes inflated by our own anger and fear.

When Sigmund Freud developed his theory of personality and psychoanalytic therapy during the first decades of the 20th Century, there was great hope that these developments would usher in a new era of enlightenment about human psychology and behavior. With such a good theory and so much more understanding of how the mind works, intense hatred and destructive behavior could be understood and controlled. Yet a few decades later, these hopes were shattered with the rise of Hitler and the Nazis who perpetrated the most heinous crimes against humanity. During World War II, Hitler and his Nazi cohorts extended the destructive power of the *Judge* from their individual psyches to all of Europe and beyond.

We believe that the concept of the *Judge* and how it operates in individual personality, family systems and in society will help you to better understand psychologically how such catastrophes can occur in highly technical and culturally advanced societies. There is a strong connection between the *Judge*, human nature, survival issues and our basic response to stress — the "fight or flight" response, our own anger and fear.

We hope that this book will provide you with a deeper understanding of the way your *Judge* may be blocking and preventing you from reaching your full potential as a human being. We also hope that it will help people with their emotional healing and recovery processes as well as with their growth towards reaching their fullest potential. Our ultimate hope is that, with this book, we can help raise people's awareness of a powerfully destructive force that operates in their individual lives and in the lives of those around them. We will also explain how you can learn to recognize this destructive force and to deflate its power over your life. We are confident that you will find that this work can be empowering for you, leading to greater emotional and spiritual growth.

Rick & Rosalie Malter

CHAPTER 1

WHAT IS THE *JUDGE*?

After a long day filled with tedious meetings and constant demands, Jeff starts his long drive home. As he navigates through the familiar streets of his hometown, he begins to sink into what he describes as the "black hole." Sometimes it feels so deep that it is like a "bottomless pit." There is absolutely no way out of it. At other times, dark clouds of depression and despair descend over Jeff, weighing him down, making him feel small and helpless. Then, suicidal thoughts start racing through his head. He feels so tense and angry that he gets the urge to just drive his car into a concrete wall and end it all. What does everyone want from him? He works hard and tries to do his best. However, it's never quite good enough. By the time he pulls into his driveway, he feels utterly drained and exhausted. He is lost in his own world of self-hate and feels overwhelmed and defeated. For Jeff, every day is a struggle just to make it through without collapsing or killing himself. He has just experienced another awful episode. He has had so many of these episodes of depression and despair. It seems like he has had them all of his life. Like all the other times, Jeff doesn't understand why the depression and hopeless despair come over him so suddenly.

Kathy has just finished meeting with her boss. He told her that her recent sales report was unsatisfactory — her sales figures were fine, but the report itself lacked sufficient detail to meet the exacting requirements of the accounting department. Kathy suddenly felt crushed. Her heart started to pound and her hands began to shake. She could feel her whole body trembling. She felt dizzy and thought she might faint.

When the brief meeting with her boss was over, she headed straight to the restroom. When she closed the door, she felt like screaming. It felt as if she were about to totally lose control of herself. She felt flooded with anxiety and had to get herself back under control. She started to do the deep breathing exercises that she'd read about in a book on panic attacks. She wondered why she wasn't calming down already. She couldn't stay in the restroom for the rest of the day. No matter how hard she tried, she couldn't stop the shaking and trembling in her body. She tried to make herself relax with the deep breathing exercises, but they didn't seem to be working for her. She thought to herself, "maybe I should try harder. Maybe I'm not breathing the right way. I always mess things up." Kathy could not comprehend what had just happened to her so suddenly. In her mind, she knew that her reaction was way out of proportion to her boss's mild reprimand. She was unable to hear the whole message from him, including, "your sales figures are fine." Still, the intensity of her panic attack left her frozen in fear. Her mind had suddenly gone blank and her panic reaction rendered her unable to think clearly and to reason things out. It felt like they had just given her the most devastating criticism of her life.

How could such a reaction happen to her? She is intelligent and can logically figure out solutions to so many problems in her life. She constantly analyzes what goes wrong with her in these types of situations. Yet, with all of her intelligence, she still can't control her emotions. Something awful must be wrong with her.

Both Jeff and Kathy have just experienced an encounter with their *Judge,* a part of their personality that developed a long time ago during their childhood years. How could this *Judge* component of personality possibly make them feel so awful after so many years? After all, they are both very bright, intelligent, and competent adults. They do so many things well and they are very successful. Yet, they suddenly wind up feeling like vulnerable helpless children. One of them was deep in depression and hopeless despair with thoughts of suicide; the other was shaking and trembling in utter panic, unable to think clearly and to cope with stress.

If Jeff and Kathy had learned how to look inside themselves, they would have discovered that there is something deep within their psychological makeup that brings on depression, panic attacks, and low self-esteem. What we have found that is so significant in many cases of depression and panic attack is that the *Judge* can be a constant source of stress for a person. The *Judge* triggers an intense stress response by its psychological effect. As we will explain in more detail later in the book, we believe that the strong psychological effect of the *Judge* is the result of its domination of a person's *inner child*, outside conscious awareness. When the *Judge* is constantly active psychologically, the resulting stress can have a continuous adverse effect on a person's biochemistry and on moods and behavior.

For most people, the *Judge* is psychologically accessible and can be confronted and defused, reducing its power and control over people's lives. Later in the book, we will go into more detail about how to access, confront and defuse the *Judge*. But, some people may be unable or unwilling to do the necessary "*Judge*-work" to free their *inner child*. Some people want a "quick-fix" solution to an uncomfortable problem. Any drug or medication or alcohol will do as long as it numbs the pain, the depression, and the terror that *the Judge* triggers. Still others refuse to look at their psychological issues and to deal with them.

There is also a quality of life issue. When the *Judge* dominates you, the quality of your life is diminished because of the limitations and emotional blocks set up by the *Judge*. It attempts to block you from developing more of your full potential as a human being. While it is blocking you, it is also taking a toll on your energy by increasing your stress level. The longer that your *Judge* is actively in control of your life, the more stress you will experience, even if it is outside your awareness.

Today, when there is such widespread use of antidepressant medications like Prozac or Zoloft, we often hear that depression and panic attacks are really only biochemical imbalances. Take a pill and that will magically fix the problem. Of course, there may, in fact, be a biochemical factor related to these psychological reactions. We also know that a flare-up of your *Judge* can trigger an intense stress response. And we know that the intensity of stress does alter a person's biochemistry. Throughout the book, we will be emphasizing the strong relationship between the mind and the body, especially when we consider the nature of the basic stress response that some of you know as the "fight or flight" response.

We all have an inner *Judge* part of our adult personality. The *Judge* is formed from an accumulation of criticism and punishment we experienced as small children from adult authority figures. Some of us had extremely traumatic and punitive experiences with raging alcoholic parents. Some of us had angry, demanding teachers. They heaped criticism and humiliation on us. Some of these adult authority figures were quietly angry and their icy cold stares would cut through us like sharp laser beams. These childhood experiences with angry, hostile, disapproving, or highly critical adults triggered an intense stress response in us — the basic "fight or flight" response. This stress response is a fundamental part of our biological and psychological makeup. It's a survival mechanism, a part of who we are as human beings.

Problems arise for us later in life when we have difficulties coming to terms with the fact that we have basic stress reactions that have such intense emotional components. Later in this book, we will describe in more detail the way, as children, we learn to distance ourselves from our own basic feelings and stress response, especially the "fight" or anger component. Adults frequently put a judgment on a child's angry feelings — "You shouldn't be angry." or "You're bad if you get angry." Sometimes, children make a decision not to ever get angry like their mom or dad because the adults get so crazy and out of control with anger. Children decide to be better than their mom or dad by never allowing themselves to get angry which they see such as a bad or destructive reaction in people. In this way, we often lose touch with this vitally important part of ourselves — the anger part of the stress response. Later in life, coping with stress then turns out to be overwhelming for some of us because we can't deal with our own anger.

In Jeff's case, the original childhood source of his *Judge* was his abusive, alcoholic father who could go into blind rages. These were absolutely terrifying to a small sensitive child. No matter how good Jeff was or how well he did in school, he could not control his father's drunken rages. It was a hopeless situation for Jeff to cope with. He felt ashamed and depressed. He often felt that it really was all his fault. If only he wouldn't make his father so angry. Then, maybe, his father wouldn't drink so much.

For Kathy, the sources of her *Judge* were many, including a series of foster parents. A few of them were alcoholic and abused her physically and sexually. Kathy had never felt a sense of security or belonging. When she was a child, the slightest thing she did wrong would be blown way out of proportion by her mother's yelling and screaming, along with giving out painful physical punishment. Kathy was always tense and anxious, never knowing when the next blow would come. She learned to be always on guard.

For both Jeff and Kathy, the childhood trauma was extreme, with a great deal of stress and constant tension. In their adult life, the *Judge* could easily and frequently manifest, causing them both physical and mental suffering that they can neither understand nor alleviate. It does not matter that these childhood events happened long ago. Their impact still has a devastating effect through the terrifying power the *Judge* established over the *inner child* so long ago.

Now, in adulthood, the *Judge* dominates the *inner child* and exploits the memories and remnants of those childhood traumas. In the adult personality, the *Judge* dominates and controls the *inner child* deep within the person's psyche outside awareness. In some ways, this process duplicates what happened to the child behind closed doors many years before. Nobody knows what is going on. The child is all alone to suffer criticism, humiliation, shame, and abuse. There is no one there to protect the child. In the same way, in adulthood, the *inner child* is at the mercy of the *Judge's* whims. Since the *Judge* remains hidden deep within the psyche outside one's conscious awareness, the *Judge's* control and domination of the person's life will remain unchallenged and unbroken.

The *Judge* prefers to operate from deep within the psyche outside a person's awareness because it is a childhood remnant that has no real energy or power of its own. It feeds off the energy of our own anger and fear. When we see it for what it really is — an illusion — it loses the power and control we have given it. (We will soon explain this illusion in more detail.) In our view, when criticism and punishment have triggered the *Judge*, we actually experience or feel the intense feelings of panic or doom by the *inner child.* If the *Judge* remains in the unconscious, dominating and terrorizing the *inner child*, it retains great psychological power. The figure here illustrates the way in which the *inner child* feels trapped by the *Judge* looming over it.

For some people, this ominous sense of doom can become overwhelming and unbearable. It also feels inescapable. No matter what a person tries, it feels like it is always there. It can be so terrifying and depressing that it can lead to intense suicidal feelings and urges. Because this sense of doom brought on by the *Judge* almost always operates outside awareness,  there is also a deep feeling of helplessness and hopelessness. A person whom this feeling of doom has overwhelmed often believes that there is no relief from this awful feeling. The person feels condemned and believes that there is no relief or escape except suicide.

Anyone who has ever experienced a panic attack that strikes for no apparent reason has probably experienced the *Judge* in a very intense way. Anyone who has ever felt deep depression or utter hopelessness and despair, a dark cloud looming overhead with gloom and doom or a sense of sinking into a deep pit also has probably experienced the profound emotional impact of the *Judge*. Another common image associated with the ominous feeling of doom brought on by the *Judge* is a sword hanging over one's head — like the sword of Damocles. Many people wonder: What is this thing we call the *Judge* that can produce some of the most common, yet overwhelming psychological conditions like panic attack and depression?

It's All an Illusion!

The tragedy for many people is that the *Judge* which triggers this awful feeling of doom, is basically an illusion! People like Jeff, Kathy and millions of others are suffering emotionally because of an illusion. Imagine that! An illusion! The *Judge* is a psychological remnant of childhood punishment, trauma, and abuse. Still, for adults, its controlling, threatening power is not part of our objective current reality. However, the feeling of doom can be so overpowering and seem so "real" that imagining that the *Judge* is simply an illusion is hard. Neverless, it is no more real than the image of a terrifying monster on a movie screen. Of course, as we all know, the movie monsters can appear frightfully real and scare us right out of our seats — we may even have nightmares about them. We also know that movie monsters can trigger exactly the same stress response as the "real" thing. Our heart races and pounds, our hands become cold and sweaty, and we feel tense all over.

We can illustrate the psychological power of the *Judge* by recalling one of the best movies in the history of film — the *Wizard of Oz*. A major part of its great popular appeal was that it so clearly showed the essence of the *Judge* and how dramatically we can unmask its illusionary nature. Throughout the film, little Dorothy and her friends are terrified and intimidated by tales of the *Wizard's* awesome power. When they finally confront the "powerful" *Wizard*, they still cower in fear and terror. His deep voice booms and bellows with demands and threats. There are much noise and smoke that add to his powerful intimidating aura. When this terrifying encounter with the *Wizard* is at its peak, Dorothy's little dog, Toto, runs over to the curtain behind which the *Wizard* is hidden and grabs the curtain with his mouth. Toto pulls the curtain open and unmasks the *Wizard*. To the amazement of Dorothy and her friends, what is revealed behind the curtain is not an all powerful *Wizard*, but only an old man grinding away at his machines and his gadgets in order to provide the illusion of having great powers. When Dorothy and her friends are able to see what is really behind the *Wizard*, they feel a great sense of relief. The *Wizard* really has no great power to control and to terrorize them anymore. Nor does he have the power to grant their wishes.

Part of the genius of this great film work is that it captured the essence of the *Judge* to which everyone can relate. The film also showed, through the actions of a frisky little dog, how easily and decisively the illusionary power of the *Judge* (as *Wizard*) can be unmasked. Later, we will explain how a similar process can occur in psychotherapy to unmask and deflate the *Judge*.

When the *Judge* is fully activated psychologically by stress, it is very much like the looming images in the old Fuji film commercials on TV. These commercials gave us the feeling of moving at high speed toward an almost certain collision with an object like a big boat or a blimp. But at the point of impact, we would suddenly tear through the paper with no harm done. What a sense of relief we would feel! There was really nothing dangerous there, but just a very realistic looking image photographed with Fuji film and printed on Fuji paper. When facing it head-on, it seemed so enormous, threatening, and powerfully real; yet, at the instant of collision and impact, it turned out to be only an image printed on very thin paper. It was easy to burst through it with no harm or real danger. Yet, from the head-on perspective of the viewer, the boat looked so overwhelmingly large and appeared to be dangerously real.

Similarly, the *Judge* is "printed" as an image in our mind in such a way that its image and verbal messages seem real and overpowering to our *inner child*. Nevertheless, the *Judge* image is only an illusion that is really paper thin, although the *inner child* doesn't know this. It sees the *Judge* from a "head-on" perspective that looks terrifying and real. If we are overwhelmed by panic and terror, we may become so intimidated that the direct confrontation and contact with the *Judge* never takes place. We may avoid this confrontation by becoming addicted to alcohol, drugs, work, gambling, sex, etc. Addictions numb our feelings or distract us. Therefore we don't feel so bad. Psychiatric medications have the same effect of helping to numb us, allowing us to avoid a confrontation with the *Judge*. When addictions or medications are used, the illusionary power of the *Judge* is never confronted and challenged. It remains intact in its full psychological intensity and control over our life. Therefore, we never discover that the terrifying overpowering *Judge* image is really a paper thin illusion. It is only by confronting this powerful psychological illusion that we learn to claim our personal power as strong capable adult human beings.

While the *Judge* is printed as an image in our mind in the same way that a monster image is printed on the movie screen, the psychological image is really an illusion that is literally paper thin. We have seen our clients make a drawing of their *Judge*. When they look at their own *Judge* drawing, whether it is very artistic or just a simple stick figure, it is truly amazing to see how anxious and fearful an adult can suddenly become when confronting the *Judge* in the drawing. Although the adult made the paper thin drawing, to the *inner child*, the head-on perspective of seeing the *Judge* image can bring on intense anxiety and panic. The person's body may recoil with a great amount of tension. A common response is that the intense stress reaction to their own *Judge* drawing feels "weird." They find it hard to believe that their simple drawing could stir up such an intense emotional response, yet they know it really happened to them. But then, they also recognize the great feeling of relief when the *Judge's* impact is diminished.

If children are shown an inflatable monster that can be pushed over, or a picture that can be torn in half, they will generally come to understand that the monster is powerless and harmless. However, if the child is filled with panic and terror, then he or she may never be willing to try to rip the picture in half or to push the fake monster over — and, the image retains its dangerous threatening aura. This is exactly the situation that many adults face today with the *Judge* outside conscious awareness.

In adulthood, the *Judge* may be viewed as a dominating figure looming over the *inner child* in a close link or bond from childhood. The *Judge* is like the paper monster that continues to look so overwhelming that it is never confronted and shown to be just an illusion. It really has no present day power of its own. It just looks scary until it is confronted and defused of its illusionary power. In fact, it is always fascinating to see that when a person gets up enough courage to confront the *Judge's* image, as its scariness diminishes, the person breathes a great sigh of relief. Many clients usually start to smile or laugh. They feel such relief! They can't believe that such a paper thin illusion has dominated their life for so many years, but now, it feels like a tremendous burden has been lifted from their shoulders.

Unfortunately, the *Judge* is an all-too-common element in numerous emotional and psychological problems affecting the lives of millions of people throughout our country. While the *Judge* can be objectively defined and described using clinical and common verbal terms, such words alone do not begin to convey the overwhelming psychological impact of the *Judge*. You can only experience the *Judge* in a personal, subjective way. In other words, there are different levels of "knowing" a psychological concept. You can know the *Judge* in an intellectual way by using descriptive words and a clinical definition. Nevertheless, by its very nature, this is a very limited way of knowing a psychological concept like the *Judge*. Experiencing one's *Judge* provides an entirely different way of knowing this type of psychological phenomenon which can dominate a person's life. Psychologists call a concept like the *Judge* a "phenomeno-logical" concept. All that really means is that it has to be subjectively experienced in order to really know it well.

"It has to be subjectively experienced in order to really know it well."

Whom Does the *Judge* Affect?
———————— ∞∞●◑◐●∞∞ ————————

If the *Judge* is affecting your life, you'll recognize yourself throughout this book, perhaps most often in some of our clients' stories which are included. Perhaps you, like Jeff, feel trapped in a "deep hole" or in the "dark pit" syndrome, usually triggered suddenly and without an apparent reason. Or, you might experience frequent panic attacks, often triggered by something outside your conscious awareness. Perhaps you've been working in a 12-step recovery program and you've managed to stop using the addictive substance. Or, perhaps you've stopped engaging in your destructive behavior, but you find that life still isn't fulfilling the promise of recovery. Is your *Judge* preventing you from fulfilling this promise of a happier, more satisfying life of sobriety? There are many ways in which the *Judge* may be activated to block your progress. The *Judge* can control your life in subtle ways as well as in the more obvious ways we've just described. In this book, you will see how the *Judge* affects your life and the lives of those around you. You will also see how the *Judge* affects our entire society as you explore the concepts we present in this book.

As we have said before, every one of us has a *Judge* component of our adult personality. This has a lot to do with human nature — with the way we are made up physically and psychologically. It also has a lot to do with the way in which children grow and develop. The *Judge* develops out of our childhood experiences. Few, if any, people had such perfect parents, teachers, and other adults around them that the *Judge* didn't have at least some fuel to feed its development. The *Judge* is an especially strong personality component in people who have been raised by very abusive adults in dysfunctional families or institutional settings.

"The *Judge* is an especially strong personality component in people who have been raised by very abusive adults in dysfuntional families or institutional settings."

Unfortunately, the *Judge* is also found in millions of people who have invested tremendous time and energy in one or more of the numerous treatment and recovery programs. However, though many recovering people find that life does improve with sobriety, their low self-esteem, fear and even depression remain pretty much unchanged. This can be very frustrating and baffling to many people after so much time, effort and money have been invested in bringing about basic life changes. Other people who have spent years in intensive psychotherapy may still find themselves psychologically stuck after putting forth so much effort. They have learned a great deal about themselves and their problems, but they seem unable to progress beyond a certain point. They still feel blocked by "something" in their lives. Henry felt such a block and described it as a "wall." When he took a closer look, he discovered that this "wall" was, psychologically, the face of his depressed father. Lauren is another person who felt blocked and stuck emotionally.

Lauren grew up in a highly dysfunctional family with a cold, controlling, and rejecting mother. As a child, she felt lost, rejected, and abandoned. She also experienced a great deal of emotional pain with these issues. At times, life felt hopeless and unbearable. She developed a severe eating disorder in order to give herself some solace and comfort from the acute emotional pain that always seemed to be with her. Her relationships always ended with deep hurt, frustration, and more emotional pain. Finally, when she no longer could tolerate her miseries, she began a treatment program for her eating disorder. She also spent nearly 10 years in various types of counseling, psychotherapy, and psychiatric treatment with many different medications. She learned a great deal about herself and her dysfunctional family life through all of her therapy and recovery work. But, much to her dismay, even though she felt better emotionally, on a physical level, she also felt exhausted. She was diagnosed with chronic fatigue syndrome and tried many approaches to restore her energy, also a very discouraging and frustrating process. She felt stuck with little hope of raising her basic energy level. Finally, she found a nutritional supplement program which gave her a significant boost in her energy. Yet ironically, as her energy level increased, she began to experience more of the old miserable feelings of low self-esteem, depression, hopelessness, intense anxiety, and panic. She was overwhelmed with the realization that she had wasted all of that time, energy, and money on recovery, therapy, and psychiatric medications. The thought occurred to her that she must really be a hopeless case if, after all these years, nothing really helped her. Her *Judge* now had ideal evidence from her ten years of therapy, recovery, and psychiatric medications that she was truly hopeless and crazy.

In fact, as we will explain in a later chapter, continuing with the traditional "talk" therapies and psychiatric medications may actually make some people worse off. After all, Lauren had done all the "right" things by going into therapy and recovery. She took her medications as her psychiatrist told her to, and she kept working and working on herself. She learned so much therapeutic information and "jargon" that she believed that she should be much better off than she actually felt. But, unbeknownst to her (on a conscious level), the harder she worked in therapy and recovery to improve her lot in life, the more she stirred up the wrath of her *Judge* which was still buried deep within her psyche. What many people like Lauren may be unaware of is that, psychologically, the *Judge* is still holding their *inner child* hostage. Every time a person like Lauren crosses a certain point in therapy, the *Judge* attacks her *inner child* and makes it pay a very high emotional price in the form of depression, panic attacks, obsessive compulsions, addictions, or self-doubt.

Some of you will be able to easily grasp this concept of the *Judge* and it will make a lot of sense to you. You will be able to apply it very effectively to your own life situation — relationships, school, athletic performance, artistic performance, work, leisure, etc. In effect, some of you will be able to do your own *Judge*-work without professional help. Others will need professional guidance and support to successfully confront and defuse the power the *Judge* has over their lives. This is an individual matter and depends to a large extent on your own unique circumstances.

How We Began Working with the *Judge* Concept
—————— ⠿⠿⠿⠿⠿⠿ ——————

In the mid-1970's, we were first introduced to the *Judge* concept by Dr. John Cooper and his colleagues at the Institute for the Natural Person (INP) in Chicago, Illinois. At first, we thought it was just an interesting variation of Freud's concept of the superego in his personality theory or a variation of the *Critical Parent* in Transactional Analysis. In other words, we believed that this was just another term for the same concept. However, we soon had personal and professional experiences that taught us that there is a major difference between the *Judge* and other psychological concepts that seem so similar to it.

For example, only a certain part of the Freudian superego is pathological. There are some positive components to the superego — a developed healthy conscience and standards of behavior. But, the *Judge* is totally pathological; it has no positive useful purpose. This is one of the major distinctions between the *Judge* and the Freudian *superego*. Since the *Judge* is totally pathological and its purpose is destructive, it is intensely related to stress on a deep emotional level. Psychologically, the *Judge* is experienced subjectively. That is, it is very personally experienced. Each person has his or her own unique *Judge*. (In psychology, this is referred to as a phenomenological experience.) It is formed in childhood from entirely negative experiences of punishment, criticism, humiliation, shame, guilt, abuse, and the stress that goes along with such psychological trauma.

Shortly after we met Dr. Cooper and his INP colleagues, we each had an opportunity to work on our own *Judge* as a part of our personal therapy and training at INP. That experience taught us a great deal about the nature of the *Judge*. The intensity of the anxiety and terror triggered by the *Judge* can only really be known from *personal* experience. No article, no book — not even this one — can possibly provide the *experiential* knowledge of the *Judge* because of its subjective nature. These words can provide an intellectual description of the *Judge*. But, from our own experience and the experiences of our clients, we know that the essence of the *Judge* is really learned on a deep feeling level. To feel the emotional impact of the *Judge* is to really know its devastating effects. To experience the feeling of relief when the *Judge* has finally been confronted and deflated is to really become free, emotionally and spiritually.

"To feel the emotional impact of the *Judge* is to really know its devastating effects. To experience the feeling of relief when the *Judge* has finally been confronted and deflated is to really become free, emotionally and spiritually."

Exposing the *Judge*

So, doesn't everyone have some experience with the *Judge?* Yes, we've all been criticized, punished, or graded and evaluated. We believe that everyone in our highly addictive, *Judge*-dominated society has some experience with the *Judge*. Yet, if that is so, why would it be such a unique and important concept in psychology today? The fact of the matter is that until we have a name for it, most of us are not fully aware of what it is that we are experiencing when we get depressed or go into a panic attack. We know the feelings can be awful — emotional pain, anxiety and panic, deep depression, feeling worthless, overwhelming guilt and shame. When these feelings become extremely intense, they may lead to suicidal or even homicidal urges. We know that our self-esteem and self-confidence might continue to be low no matter what we do to try to change ourselves. We may not understand why relationships within our families, schools, workplaces, organizations, and even places of worship seem to trigger these intense feelings of panic, depression, and despair. In fact, we believe that wherever one finds rigid rules and regulations which are enforced in a cold, uncaring, and dogmatic way, a *Judge* is not far away.

In recent years, a number of concepts have emerged that touch on some of the ways that the *Judge* component manifests in personality development and the way we function as adults. When author and lecturer John Bradshaw talks about "toxic shame" originating in dysfunctional family systems and carrying over into adult life, he is identifying one of the major effects of the *Judge*. As you will see, the emphasis on the *inner child* is also related to the *Judge*. (Dr. Charles Whitfield has written extensively on the concept of the *Inner Child*.) We have also found that the Warrior archetype in Jungian psychology can be meaningfully related to the *Judge*. In therapy, Warrior energy is very powerful in confronting and defusing the *Judge's* illusionary power over the *inner child*. We will explain this in more detail later in the book.

The *Judge* and the *Inner Child*

The *Judge* is both insatiable and inconsistent. Children who are raised in dysfunctional families, or schools, or neighborhoods will always feel vulnerable to behavior that is inconsistent, threatening, and unpredictable. We have all heard people say that they tried to figure out what their alcoholic or raging parent really wanted. "Whatever it was, I'd have done it," one of our clients said, "but there was no way to know from one day to the next what my father wanted from us. Whatever we did, it was either wrong or not good enough. There was no way to win. It was impossible to do anything right."

This unpredictability and the inconsistency are a crazy making system because you are never sure of what is really expected no matter what you do or how hard you try. Some children just give up and withdraw into apathy and depression. Other children become so tense and anxious, they sometimes can't even think straight. Children in an environment like this will feel intense emotional stress because the parent — and, later, the internal *Judge* — is always ready to strike at any time. But the child never knows when the next strike will come. Such children learn to become hypervigilant, always wary and on guard. Vigilance is their key to survival in a very hostile and threatening environment. Is it any wonder that a person coming from this type of environment will feel anxious and tense much of the time? The person is set up in childhood to develop a very strong dominating *Judge*. As children, they make a deal with their developing *Judge* for protection if they become perfect, or quiet, or don't make waves.

Panic attacks and depression are common reactions when the *Judge* causes the person to feel that every action or even one's thoughts are constantly scrutinized for the slightest flaw. No action or thought is ever really good enough. The *Judge* demands perfection and that's all that is acceptable. Anything less than perfect is worthless! This helps to explain the phenomenon of the highly successful person who still suffers from a strong sense of inadequacy and self-doubt. How much is enough to ever satisfy the insatiable demands of the *Judge*? Huge salaries, advanced college degrees, "trophy" spouses, lavish lifestyles, devotion to volunteer service, selfless giving, and so forth, will never be enough to fill the bottomless pit that the *Judge* keeps us in with its critical and destructive messages. Understanding this helps us begin the work of reducing or lessening the hold that the *Judge* has on us.

One of the first things the *Judge* will do is to attempt to thwart the work that will unmask it and help to loosen its grip on a person's life. Remember, that is the main job of the *Judge* — to keep a tight grip on your "life script." This is a concept described by Claude Steiner in his book *Scripts People Live*. A person may act as if he or she were following a "script," which says, for example, "I am worthless" and "I must be *super* competent to prove I'm not worthless." All of the *Judge* messages form the basis of this "life script." Depending on how strong the messages are, they can be just mildly troubling or extremely destructive (a "tragic script") leading to addictions of all sorts, chronic pain, suicide, or homicide. If you depart from your life script, this will stir the wrath of the *Judge*. Its job is to tell you that, no matter what you do, no matter how good it is, you are shamefully and fatally flawed. It demands perfection, but it tries to always find a flaw in you, no matter how minute or miniscule. It inflates the flaw to massive proportions.

One of the bewildering aspects of modern psychotherapy is that extensive work and dedication on the part of the client doesn't always bring positive results. Sally, a 40-year-old woman, had come to us for help with her lifelong depression. Over a 10-year period, she had been given more than 15 different medications, none of which worked very well, except to dull her feelings and to confuse her. She also had spent a number of years in "verbal" psychotherapy. With all of her work in therapy, and with all of her different medications, she still fluctuated between deep depression and panic attacks. Unfortunately, this is all too common in the mental health field.

Since Sally was quite bright, she had learned a great deal about herself and a lot of therapy "jargon." Because she was bright and had learned much in therapy, she also felt an overwhelming sense of failure as a human being. How could she have gained so much personal knowledge and "insight" and still feel so awful about herself? Her *Judge* had gathered much additional evidence to use against her. After all these years of medication and therapy, she still felt miserable. She came to the conclusion that she must really be sick and hopeless as a human being!

Sally also was an adult child of an alcoholic parent (ACOA) and a recovering alcoholic herself. Although she became sober and maintained her sobriety, she felt uncomfortable at AA meetings because she still felt terrible about herself. The more she tried to figure out and analyze what was wrong with her, the more confused she became. This reinforced her feeling that she was "dumb" and "stupid." One of her deepest fears was that she was "crazy." This made perfectly good sense to her because she had been depressed all of her life. After all, a number of psychiatrists had tried all kinds of antidepressants on her with no substantial improvement or lasting results. This surely proved to her *Judge* and to all of these psychiatrists that she was truly "crazy." Her *Judge* told her that she must really be a "hopeless" case because recovery in AA, antidepressants, and so many years of psychotherapy had produced no significant improvement in her chronic depression and low self-esteem. She seemed to feel constantly angry and resentful that no program or therapist was good enough to cure her or make her feel better about herself.

Sally would feel a sense of "doom" all the time. She was afraid she would die at any moment and felt like she walked around in a dark cloud. Life felt "bleak" and "dismal." She felt that somebody was back there in her head beating her. She felt bad, stupid, worthless, and ugly, and always was on the defensive. She had an intense inner conflict. There was this "thing," she said, "that won't let me change and it is stronger than the part in me that wants to change. It's a black thing that holds on to me and holds everything down." It says, "You're really dumb! You're trying to play a game. Nothing is real." She became so terrified that she wanted to stop and run away. But, it's impossible to run away from the *Judge*. We always take it with us no matter where we go.

Sally describes many *Judge* characteristics. Experientially, she had felt its impact and how it dominated her entire life. Yet because the *Judge* was operating outside her awareness and had such a tight grip on her *inner child,* she thought there was no escape. She felt doomed, trapped, and in utter despair and misery. She also did not realize that the intensity of her own anger and rage kept her *Judge* fully inflated so it could continue to dominate and control her entire life. This is a crucial point in understanding the nature of the *Judge*. It always feeds off the energy produced by our own stress reaction — the "fight or flight" response. The energy generated by our own anger or fear is what inflates the *Judge* deep within our psyche. The *Judge* has no psychological energy or power of its own. It is a parasite which terrorizes our *inner child* so that it can feed off the energy associated with our own fear and anger.

Even though Sally knew the *Judge*'s impact well through her own experience, it did her no good psychologically because nobody had ever explained to her what her experience was all about. Nobody had helped her to make sense of what she was so painfully aware of in her psychological experience. In fact, her feelings and experiences were used to "diagnose" her as chronically depressed and in need of medication to cure her "mental illness."

Actually, we find that Sally's case isn't at all unusual. Many people spend years searching, analyzing, and trying to figure out their lives, but they still run up against the overwhelming *Judge*. Like Sally, they, too, were worried that they were crazy or were too sick to be helped. Unfortunately, Sally's work with her therapists had served to reinforce the idea that she was a hopeless case, although she had made an adjustment to her chronic depression. If things were going reasonably well in her life, she could at least cope and hang on. On the outside, she looked relatively animated and bright. But, on the inside, she felt numb and dead. It seemed as if a 100-pound weight was pressing down on her neck and shoulders. What a depressing burden! If things weren't going well or if she faced a major change in her life, then the panic attacks would start and she felt alone and terrified. "I can't handle those simple things that responsible normal adults just take in stride," Sally said. "Even buying a house, which should be an exciting and happy event, fills me with overwhelming anxiety and terror. What if I am making a mistake?" Doubts start to take her over. "I just don't want to live like this anymore." The doubts escalate and she becomes immobilized with the fear of making the wrong decision. Any mistake becomes catastrophic to her.

One of the first impressions we had of Sally was that she was very bright and intuitive. She also expressed herself with very clear visual imagery. She had considerable awareness of her own sensations and feelings. However, she had learned to dismiss these feelings and images as evidence of her wild imagination and "craziness." In fact, she was very *visual* and *kinesthetic* in her descriptions of her experiences. These are ideal traits for dealing with the *Judge*. Over the years, she had learned to discount these traits which could be powerful tools in therapy and recovery.

On some level, Sally was aware of the *Judge*, but for her and for most people, the *Judge* is not very well defined or clear because it usually operates outside awareness. She had a clear sense of the feelings associated with it — depression, hopelessness, despair, anxiety, and panic attacks. Its ominous threats of doom and domination seemed to appear without warning and with no apparent trigger. Jeff's *Judge* also operates that way. There he was, just driving home from a busy day at the office when all of a sudden, the *Judge* raised its ugly head and lowered the boom, so to speak. He just couldn't understand why this happened and what was really going on deep inside his psyche.   Kathy's panic attack was triggered by what, objectively, was a minor incident. The problem is, once the panic attack began, her ability to think and to reason was all, but gone. Her thoughts and feelings escalated out of her control. The slightest criticism devastated her. If Kathy tried to analyze the incident itself and convinced herself that the whole thing was silly, then the *Judge* would just strike again over another minor incident. This is the way the *Judge* operates. It waits for its opportunity and then it zaps the person, coming from out of nowhere. It operates like a hit-and -run driver. It smacks you and then it disappears, leaving you in shock, depression, or panic.

"...she was very *visual* and *kinesthetic* in her descriptions of her experiences. These are ideal traits for dealing with the *Judge*."

The *Judge* is Everywhere

As you will see later, the *Judge* can operate anywhere and everywhere. Clint Black, the popular country singer, recently wrote and recorded a song, *One Emotion*, which expresses this idea very well. We would paraphrase the lyrics and say that we always take our *Judge* with us "no matter where we go." There are *Judge*-dominated people everywhere we go. These individuals can affect you at school, at work, in your community activities, as well as in your closest intimate relationships. There may be *Judge*-dominated people in the health care professions or in 12-step recovery groups. If you go to a psychiatrist or a psychotherapist, you may encounter the *Judge* part of the professional's personalities. Later, we will describe how the *Judge* may come out in a 12-step group. We will also describe how the *Judge* operates in a patient-doctor relationship. Remember, the *Judge* is a part of the human condition — it's a part of everyone's psyche.

As you will discover later in the book, there are some people whose *Judge* is only a very small part of their personalities. Their sensitivity, creativity, and spirituality are clear and apparent in every aspect of their lives. Their aliveness and their love is their very essence. It seems that everyone and everything they touch comes alive with their warmth and their spirit. They are warm, spontaneous, and loving.

Then, at the opposite extreme, there are some people whose *Judge* seems to totally dominate their personality and everything they do. They appear to be emotionally flat and lifeless. They are two-dimensional because life has crushed their spirit and left them flattened — emotionally dead. They may be very bright and intelligent, but, emotionally, they are dead. They often have a gray pallor to their skin. Their eyes are dull and vacant as if "nobody is home." They don't feel anything. They are cut off from their bodies and their feelings.

These types of people can send a cold chill up your spine. If that is the way your body reacts to this type of *Judge*-dominated person, then pay close attention to your body's reaction. Your body is picking up the icy cold "vibe" of this type of a *Judge*. Your body's intuitive response knows that this type of *Judge* is very destructive in a quiet calculating way. In emotionally dead people, it is as if their *Judge* has spread through their bodies like an emotional cancer, completely taking them over. In fact, a *Judge* that is dominant and unchecked in a person can be as deadly as cancer.

"...a *Judge* that is dominant and unchecked in a person can be as deadly as cancer."

If you have been in the presence of a highly *Judge*-dominated person, you also know well what that feels like experientially. Such a *Judge*-dominated person could be a parent, a boss, a business or professional colleague, a helping professional such as a doctor or psychologist, a person of the clergy, or a teacher. In the presence of such a person, you feel unusually tense, "on guard", not sure of yourself, chronically anxious and insecure, and extremely vulnerable. No matter what you do, it will always be open to criticism, ridicule, never quite "good enough.".

Unfortunately, large numbers of people spend virtually their entire lifetime in the presence of such *Judge*-dominated persons. Many people work for or are married to such a person. Whole families are dominated by such people. That is one of the main reasons why some family gatherings are so tension filled and traumatic, especially at holiday gatherings and other major family events. Alcoholic and other highly dysfunctional families are very *Judge*-dominated.

"You can be both the <u>victim</u> of another person's *Judge* and the <u>perpetrator</u> using your own *Judge* to criticize, control, and dominate another person."

You can be both the <u>victim</u> of another person's *Judge* and the <u>perpetrator</u> using your own *Judge* to criticize, control, and dominate another person. When you are being influenced by your *Judge*, then strong authority figures will constantly seem to be making excessive demands and pressuring you. No matter how well you do your school work or perform your job tasks, no matter how much you help others, or sacrifice yourself for friends or family or the community, it is never good enough to satisfy the *Judge*. You will always fall short because the *Judge* uses an <u>elastic</u> standard of performance. It always changes just when you think you are close to perfection. As long as your *Judge* operates deep within your psyche, outside of your awareness, you can never really win or succeed. It always demands more and more until it wears you down. Nobody can possibly have enough energy to keep working towards satisfying the insatiable demands of the *Judge*. You will eventually totally exhaust yourself trying to meet its standards of absolute perfection. And, while you are striving towards achieving such absolute perfection, you will find that you have lost total control over your own life. This will also leave you wide open and vulnerable to addictions and codependent behavior. As this is happening to you, you may find yourself being more and more demanding and judgmental towards others around you. Your children might say, "I can't win around here. If I get a B+, you want to know why it's not an A." Or, your colleagues might lament, "Hey, we're all giving 150% to this project, and it's never enough. All you do is demand more and more. Nothing ever satisfies you."

The *Judge* is an Anti-Life Force

Dr. Deepak Chopra, Physician, often talks about the potentialities in life that may fill us with joy and love and happiness. But, there is also a phenomenon which he and others call *entropy* that works against the human spirit and the tendency towards wholeness. As a person works in therapy, in recovery, or on personal or spiritual growth, the *Judge* will attempt to block any significant progress. If you have ever experienced this type of block, then the *Judge* has attacked your desire to be more alive, more creative, more spontaneous, and more filled with the joy of living. One client told us that after attending a weekend seminar on setting goals and reaching them he actually felt worse. His feelings of worthlessness and doom intensified, and he fell into a familiar deep suicidal depression. We believe that this illustrates a classic *Judge* attack, trying to frighten and intimidate the person so that he will avoid a positive enriching experience.

"The *Judge's* control over our life script is threatened whenever we attempt to change — to move forward and to enrich our lives."

The *Judge's* control over our life script is threatened whenever we attempt to change — to move forward and to enrich our lives. Often, when we have consciously chosen to engage in something positive and life enhancing, the *Judge's* wrath is stirred. An unconscious confrontation occurs deep within our psyche, and it often escalates and intensifies. If you are unaware of the phenomenon of the *Judge*, you are at a great disadvantage when this confrontation occurs. You will feel that "something" has taken hold of you, but you won't know what it is or understand it because it caught you off guard and you are completely on the defensive. You don't even know who or what you are fighting. It's like fighting a psychological guerilla war on somebody else's terms and territory.

Next, we will take a look at how the *Judge* develops during childhood and at what factors contribute to its development in our personalities.

CHAPTER 2

HOW THE *JUDGE* DEVELOPS IN CHILDHOOD

A friend of ours recently described a situation in which her very bright 8-year-old son had difficulty dealing with a change in plans. Our friend had explained to her son that they would be stopping at the chiropractor's office for about 45 minutes, then they would go shopping and do a few other things. The boy understood what the plan was and he was prepared to sit and wait for 45 minutes while his mother had her chiropractic treatment. However, since the chiropractor was a half hour behind schedule, our friend realized that this would no longer fit with her tight schedule and she would have to arrange for another appointment. Her son was very upset that the plan had changed and said, "But, mom, you said we would be here for forty-five minutes. That's OK with me. I brought my book along. I can wait." He had a great deal of difficulty dealing with the sudden change of plans. This is a very natural reaction by an 8-year-old child, typical of his stage of development.

For 8-year-old children, life follows a rigid set rules and expectations. Children's games have to be played according to certain rigid rules and there are no exceptions. Children also insist that the game has to be played their way. The child's mind cannot reconcile opposites — everything is "either-or, but not both"; things are just different, that's all. The important point here is that the child's concrete mode of thinking also becomes the mode of the *Judge's* thinking. However, this doesn't mean that the child is *Judge*-dominated. The behavior is appropriate to that developmental level. Every one of us goes through this natural stage of development, and 8-year-old children go through this rigid, dogmatic stage of child development. Nevertheless, it is quite a different situation if you are dealing with an adult who is operating from a *Judge*-dominated place. When that happens, the adult is functioning, psychologically, from an 8-year-old place. This mental level is out of step with the adult body. Later in the book, we will explain more about this split between the immature mental level of the *Judge* and the adult body.

"...children's experience of reality is highly circumscribed and distorted. Exceptions to the rules are difficult and frustrating for them to cope with. The uncertainties, the gray areas, and the contradictions in life are conveniently overlooked, discounted, and ignored. This lays the foundation for the *modus operandi* of the *Judge*."

From the concrete view of the 8-year-old, reality is understood to have absolute certainty — no doubt about it. Emotionally, 8-year-olds are still subject to childhood dependency, insecurities, anxiety, and vulnerability. The belief in absolute certainty is very comforting to children. At this stage of development, children have no conceptual system for dealing with contradictory information and uncertainty — the gray areas. Therefore, children are highly selective about what observations, information, and data they allow into the system. Thus, children's experience of reality is highly circumscribed and distorted. Exceptions to the rules are difficult and frustrating for them to cope with. The uncertainties, the gray areas, and the contradictions in life are conveniently overlooked, discounted, and ignored. This lays the foundation for the *modus operandi* of the *Judge*.

Formation of the *Judge*
—————— ∞◐◑∞ ——————

The *Judge* and its formation in personality development are part of the organic processes of life. By that we mean that it forms through an accumulation of experiences in childhood that are blended with a child's perceptions, thoughts, memories, and physiological sensations, especially those associated with the "fight or flight" stress response. When the *Judge* splits off in personality development, usually when a child is between eight and ten years old, it splits with an experiential *matrix* that contains perceptions, thoughts, memories, and physiological sensations. An experiential matrix is a mix of all these factors. The way these factors mix is unique to each person so that every person has his or her own unique *Judge*. This is why it is experienced in a highly subjective way. One person's image or symbol of their *Judge* may trigger intense panic or terror, yet this image or symbol may have very little or no effect on another person.

The development of the *Judge* is strongly related to certain factors that are inherently related to the human condition in general and to child development in particular. Punishing and traumatizing experiences — yelling and screaming at a child or slapping a child — contribute to the development of the *Judge*. These are strongly connected to the basic stress response — the "fight or flight" response. Therefore, the *Judge* can easily trigger an intense stress response and keep a person in a chronic state of high stress, but outside a person's own awareness. The human nervous and glandular systems are strongly connected to the psyche. This is evident in the stress response. The human neuro-psychological system is "wired" so that it is conducive to developing the *Judge* component in a person's personality.

There is another important aspect of child development that plays a major role in the formation of the *Judge* component in personality development. This aspect has to do with the concrete type of thinking which characterizes the young child. The child thinks in terms of absolutes, opposite poles, either-or, black or white, good or bad, right or wrong. The young child hasn't matured enough to be able to think in terms of the gray areas of life, nor can the child deal with contradictory or incompatible conditions if new circumstances arise.

When there is a great deal of dysfunction in the family — alcoholism, chronic illness or disability in a family member, poor communication,

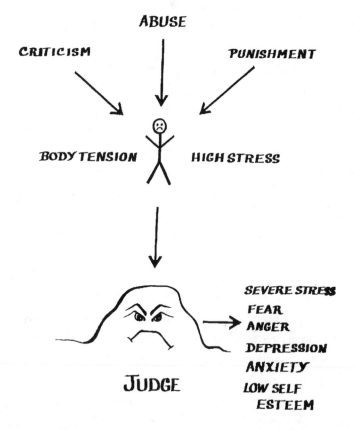

ADULT ANGER AND RAGE

ABUSE

CRITICISM   **PUNISHMENT**

BODY TENSION   **HIGH STRESS**

SEVERE STRESS
FEAR
ANGER
DEPRESSION
ANXIETY
JUDGE   **LOW SELF**
ESTEEM

constant yelling and screaming, corporal punishment, physical, emotional, or sexual abuse, etc. — then children will feel chronic tension and high stress levels. These are some highly stressful psychological conditions that will intensify the formation of the *Judge* in children.

A *Judge* "Attack"

Fred, at 19 years of age, described what it was like to grow up with the constant stress from his raging, abusive, *Judge*-dominated dad:

"If dad were upset, he would have anger fits. Then he'd go to his room. He would become very quiet, but gave out an angry stare. He wouldn't say anything. When dad was silent, I couldn't tell how angry he really was. When he was loud and more explosive, it was easy to tell. He had the coldest stare. When he was silent, I didn't know when the big explosion was coming. It was like stepping through a minefield. His silence made me more nervous than when he actually exploded. The silence was worse because I didn't know."

The long-term effect on Fred was that he had an extremely intense psychological and body reaction to anything or anyone who would trigger a *Judge* attack in him. The intensity of his father's rage  and *Judge* was so great that the energy behind that rage would blast Fred's body and spirit. The energy of his father's *Judge*-driven rage penetrated Fred's body to the depths of his soul. The explosiveness of his father's rage penetrated deep into Fred's body, down to his very cells and tissues. Consequently, even when he was older, in his late teens or early twenties, a *Judge* attack would quickly overwhelm Fred. He would experience a *Judge* attack on a basic reflex level — in an instant. He would have feelings of intense anxiety and panic without control of body reactions

— jerking, shaking, and trembling. Although Fred was very bright, he could not voluntarily control these intense stress reactions with his strong verbal logical mind.

As he grew and matured in therapy, Fred began to become desensitized to the automatic reflex response he had to a *Judge* attack. He started to recognize the situations when his *Judge's* wrath was stirred up. "When I get close to getting what I really want," he observed, "something that is good, then the fear of 'losing it' intensifies." This is an example of the *Judge* at work in blocking us from experiencing happier, more satisfying things in life. In a later chapter on therapy, we will describe in more detail how Fred learned to defuse his terrifying *Judge* and to take greater control of his own life.

In an individual's personality, the *Judge* becomes a separate psychological entity that functions like a hologram buried deep within the psyche. A hologram is a special picture form, characterized by the fact that any part of it is capable of recreating the whole image. So, when any part of the *Judge* is triggered by a <u>stressful</u> experience, the entire *Judge* may inflate like a huge balloon and overwhelm a person. When this happens, we refer to it as a *Judge* "attack." For some people, a *Judge* attack may feel like a heart attack because the physiological reactions to the stress can be so intense. A person may feel totally overwhelmed with panic and terror for no apparent reason. For most people, this happens because the *Judge* operates outside awareness, since it is buried deep within the psyche. A *Judge* attack occurs for no apparent reason. Yet, its impact feels very real because it is so intense both psychologically and physiologically. Many people who have what is psychiatrically diagnosed as "panic disorder" are really experiencing repeated attacks of their *Judge* on their *inner child*. Depression also can result from a *Judge* attack. Later in the book, we will give more examples of how a *Judge* attack occurs and what you can do about it.

When the *Judge* is actively operating in an adult, criticizing other people is usually exaggerated. The criticism feels like overkill that often doesn't really fit the circumstances. It is important for you to be aware that even when these overly critical responses are coming from another adult, that person is operating psychologically from a child place. Don't be fooled by the fact that the criticism or put down is coming from an adult body. Remember, a put down remark is also a power play — an attempt to get one-up over you. Emotionally, the *Judge* is trying to cover up the fact that there is a very insecure and frightened *inner child* inside such a person who is trying to seem strong and in control.

"...when these overly critical responses are coming from another adult, that person is operating psychologically from a child place."

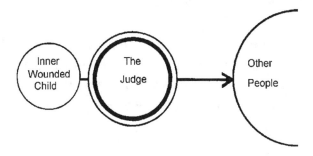

"There is always a terrified vulnerable *inner child* behind every *Judge*. The *Judge* hides this *inner child* by intimidating other people."

When this happens, notice the words the person uses. Notice the rigid, dogmatic attitude. Notice the either-or type of thinking. Then, be sure to take note of the impact that this *Judge*-dominated attitude has on your body and your feelings. Notice that it always involves a power struggle and an effort to exert control over you. This is actually the underlying situation whenever the "Peter Principle" operates in a business or institution. When people in authority have reached their level of incompetence, they get frightened and fall back on their *Judge* to intimidate and confuse their subordinates. The *inner child* in the authority figure is afraid of being found flawed and incompetent. Job stress and tension in the entire organization increase to intense levels because the *Judge* is active. A frequent outcome is that a more competent subordinate may be fired because the *inner child* of the incompetent authority feels so threatened. This is one of the most common ways in which the *Judge* can adversely affect and destabilize a previously well functioning organization.

"... note the impact that this *Judge*-dominated attitude has on your body and your feelings ... it always involves a power struggle and an effort to exert control over you."

The *Judge* Collects Evidence

To gain and maintain control, the *Judge* collects information and data, which are transformed into *evidence* to support its preconceived notions and prejudicial positions. Like the 8-year-old, the *Judge* selects only what is useful to support its position and presents its evidence as incontrovertible fact. It is very biased and prejudiced in its views. The

Judge can take the slightest flaw or error and inflate it into a major issue. We saw this in Kathy's case in the first chapter. A minor critical comment was inflated by her own *Judge* until it emotionally overwhelmed her with panic. No matter whether we are dealing with our own *Judge* internally or if we are dealing with someone else's *Judge* externally (a boss or supervisor, a spouse, a teacher, a friend, etc.), the *Judge* inflates information and data in the same way to control us by threat, intimidation, humiliation, and unfair criticism.

In interpersonal relations, this process by a *Judge*-dominated person feels to the other person like manipulation and a power play. To try to be logical and reasonable plays into the hands of the *Judge* who operates with rigid simplistic logic. In fact, when dealing with another person who is operating from a *Judge* position, the more verbal, analytical, and logical you try to be, the more frustrated and victimized you will feel. This will only feed and fuel the *Judge* even more, particularly if your frustration and anger show.

> **"To try to be logical and reasonable plays into the hands of the *Judge* who operates with rigid simplistic logic."**

The *Judge* and Intelligence

The *Judge* exists in people with very different levels of intelligence and mental abilities. Sometimes, this can lead a person to feel confused, disappointed, and even disillusioned. This reaction often happens to young people when they go off to college or to a professional school.

James was always very curious and inquisitive. From the time he was a little boy, he always asked questions and had an insatiable thirst for knowledge and explanations. He wanted to know more and more, and it was very important to him to understand how things worked. School was easy for him. He did very well from the time he was in kindergarten until he was graduated from college with honors. He was thrilled when he was accepted to five different medical schools. He chose the most prestigious school of the five, naively believing that prestige and quality were synonymous. He was excited to have several classes with distinguished professors like "Dr. Smith" who had published well-known medical textbooks and articles. Just imagine! James would have a class with the great Dr. Smith.

Nevertheless, James couldn't grasp what was happening when he asked Dr. Smith an insightful question to clarify an ambiguous point in the professor's textbook. James often got a cold angry look in response to his well-thought out question, and sometimes Dr. Smith would make a cutting or disparaging remark to James, embarrassing him in front of the entire class. He felt completely bewildered. He brought his natural curiosity and enthusiasm for learning to his medical education, and yet, when he asked questions to clarify his learning process, he was met with intense hostility. The professor was brilliant and very articulate, yet why was he so hostile to a student's honest questions? Well, perhaps an answer can be found using the *Judge* concept.

"The *Judge* pretends that intellectual knowledge is absolute and certain, although it is only an *approximation* expressed in terms of probability."

The *Judge* pretends that intellectual knowledge is absolute and certain, although it is only an approximation expressed in terms of probability. The *Judge* never wants to be challenged about its absolute certainty and authority, and will not tolerate a challenge to its rigid position. The *Judge* manipulates data to fit its preconceived notions and prejudices. If there is any new or different perspective or paradigm, the *Judge* fights any paradigm shift with all of the ploys at its command.

The *Judge* is inherently a skeptic: "Prove it to me with absolute certainty or else I won't believe you." The *Judge* has no sense of trust — it fragments off from the terrified child ego state. It dissociates from the feelings of utter terror and vulnerability by going entirely into its head, cut off from the body that has the capacity to experience the entire range of emotion. The *Judge* is literally out of touch with most aspects of experience and reality. Because it is cut off from feelings, it has no way of knowing something in an intuitive way.

"The *Judge* is literally out of touch with most aspects of experience and reality. Because it is cut off from feelings, it has no way of knowing something in an intuitive way."

Dr. Smith may have been intellectually brilliant, but emotionally he was poorly developed. Any challenge to his authority and expertise was met with hostility driven by his *Judge*. The professor's intellect and clinical knowledge were so intertwined with his *Judge* that he became insecure, rigid, and defensive whenever a student raised a question. The *Judge* cannot admit, "I don't know," "I'm not really sure," or "I'll have to think about that." This intertwining of intellect and clinical knowledge with the *Judge* created a web that could trap a student like James. This psychological web could leave him confused, disappointed and disillusioned. For all of his own high intelligence, James did not grasp the simple fact that intellectual brilliance and academic achievement do not necessarily parallel emotional and spiritual development and maturity. Many people have great intelligence and academic achievement, but are emotionally underdeveloped. In fact, this combination of high intelligence, academic achievement, and emotional underdevelopment is a fertile breeding ground for the *Judge*-domination found in so many organizations and institutions in our society, including the health care and education fields. Let's take a look to see how this can occur as often as it does.

"...intellectual brilliance and academic achievement do not necessarily parallel emotional and spiritual development and maturity."

Intuitive "Knowing"

For the most part, our educational system, wittingly or unwittingly, is designed to *train* children into dissociating from their bodies and their capacity for intuitive knowing. Children are typically trained to believe that only those experiences that can be verbally described and measured are real and represent truth. The left hemisphere functions of the brain (logical and verbal) are overemphasized and idealized while the right hemisphere (creative and intuitive) is considered frivolous and untrustworthy. Book learning and logical analysis are the only generally accepted sources of *real* knowledge. If it can be found in print, it must be true and real.

"The left hemisphere functions of the brain (logical and verbal) are over-emphasized and idealized while the right hemisphere (creative and intuitive) is considered frivolous and untrustworthy."

In contrast, *intuitive* knowing is often distrusted and considered suspect because it comes from the body and the "gut." Skeptics say that there are no hard data to measure objectively. Therefore, how could there be any truth and validity to such experiences? However, those who have learned to trust their gut and intuition know things with much more assurance and certainty than those who overanalyze and intellectualize. This gut level knowing comes from a very confident *trusting* place. This is a different kind of *knowing* from the type coming from a *Judge* place. Trust is a feeling and a sensation felt in the body. Trust is not an intellectual process.

"This often leads to very unbalanced development that disables many people psychologically."

The body's mode of *knowing* something intuitively reflects an awareness and consciousness unfamiliar to many people living in Western societies. Usually, our child rearing practices and rigid academic settings allow the child's natural curiosity, body awareness, and intuitive knowing to atrophy. In our society, most children and adolescents lose awareness of the body senses that support their intuition. They are taught to believe that only experience that can be verbally described and measured is real and represents truth. This often leads to very unbalanced development that disables many people psychologically.

How Data Become Evidence for the *Judge*

The natural human tendency is to observe, perceive, and obtain information to make functional discriminations and informed decisions. There is no inherent manipulation or power play involved in this natural human decision making process. The scientific process is the most highly refined example of this natural process. Scientific observations, data collection and information are interpreted in terms of probabilities. This process may provide an approximation of certainty, but inherently, it lacks *absolute certainty.*

Scientists who are emotionally secure understand that there are certain inherent limitations to knowing something with absolute certainty. We can probably come close to knowing and understanding something, but absolute certainty is impossible. Even in a "hard" science such as physics that uses precise measurements and data, the realities of the complex phenomena of the universe forced physicists themselves to recognize that there could be no absolutes. The great physicist, Werner Heisenberg, described the "principle of uncertainty" that is associated with his name. The very act of observing something alters its basic nature. In other words, it is impossible to be completely objective. All observation and experience have a subjective element. We can never be absolutely sure of something even with the best measurements. In many situations, we can probably come close, but not with 100 percent certainty.

In his recent book, *Chaos: Making a New Science,* James Gleick describes some fascinating recent developments in mathematics and basic science that are consistent with the view we are discussing here. The complex dynamic human system of feelings, behaviors, and body chemistry produce fluctuations in all of us that move between stability and instability. These developments transcend the simplistic notions of psychiatry and clinical psychology that you can accurately "diagnose" a mental illness and then "treat" it with either a drug or a behavioral manipulation. This simplistic approach is based on the illusion of control over this dynamic human system. Each person's system may have some similarities to that of others, but each of us has our own unique pattern that unfolds very clearly in *Judge*-work therapy. We don't control the process; it progresses and unfolds naturally, but unpredictably.

Consequently, we need to develop emotional maturity that allows us to recognize and to tolerate the uncertainties of life without going crazy with fear and panic. A corollary to this point is that there is a limit to our own control over events in life. With knowledge and technical skill, we can control a lot, but there are still limits to our power. The mature person recognizes this basic fact of life and can calmly accept it.

On the other hand, people in whom the *Judge* dominates cannot tolerate and accept limitations to their own power and control. It drives them to control everyone and everything because they are really terrified of having no control at all in their life. Therefore, they must control everything and everyone, and always have it their way. They will also twist facts and data to fit their prejudices and biases. The *Judge* can inflate a minor flaw or error into a major episode. Or, conversely, the *Judge* can minimize or dismiss something really important in a situation. Basically, the *Judge* always distorts and uses information and data for purposes of power and control over someone. Being totally in control also gives such a person the illusion of having absolute certainty and knowing what is best for everyone else. This is the classic co-dependent person who always knows what is best for everyone else.

"Basically, the *Judge* always distorts and uses information and data for purposes of power and control over someone."

Since the *Judge* always operates, psychologically, from the same place as 8-year-old children, it cannot comprehend or tolerate uncertainty. It attempts to create certainty by forcing everything into rigid absolute categories of opposite polarities — good or bad, right or wrong, black or white, etc. This is the way it tries to make sense of a very complicated world with inherent uncertainty built in.

The *Judge* creates life's "procedure manual" that tells us exactly how to live our lives in a very rigid, highly controlled manner that provides us with the illusion of having certainty and control. Our *inner child* buys into this deal with the *Judge* because, otherwise, life is too unpredictable and scary. The *inner child* makes a pact or contract with the *Judge* to comply with its insatiable and impossible demands in exchange for "protection" by the *Judge*. In effect, the *Judge* bullies the *inner child* into submitting to its threats and intimidation. In later chapters, we will explain how this outrageous psychological deal can be exposed and safely broken to free the *inner child* from domination by the *Judge*. This process will allow a person to live a much more emotionally secure, relaxed, and fulfilling life.

Some people will experience great difficulty in confronting and defusing the *Judge's* power and control over their lives. This is because of a subtle paradox involving the *Judge* and feelings. Both of Cindy's parents had a great deal of difficulty dealing with her intense feelings. She was a bright, sensitive child who had strong emotional reactions to different situations. Therefore, her parents placed their own *Judges* on her feelings, especially anger and fear. Cindy was often told, "You shouldn't feel angry!" or "There's no reason to be afraid."

Such judgmental messages about basic feelings, especially those that are automatically triggered with the stress response, led to added stress, conflict, and confusion for Cindy. Anger and fear are feeling responses that occur automatically under stressful conditions. Her parents' judgmental messages about these intense feelings put Cindy into conflict with her own natural emotional reactions. As a result, she learned to dissociate from her own feelings of anger and fear. She wouldn't allow these feelings to become a part of herself and her experience. However, hard as she tried, her body would still react to stress and produce the fight or flight response. Anger and fear were still stirred up in her regardless of whether she allowed herself to feel these emotions or not. The anger and fear also became the source of energy the *Judge* relied on to inflate itself and to exercise its intimidating power over her *inner child*. By dissociating from these basic feelings of anger and fear as an adult, it became much more difficult for Cindy to accept and to own these natural feelings and reactions as a normal part of herself. Therefore, the *Judge* was still able to draw on the energy of these feelings to inflate itself and to maintain its control over her *inner child.*

> **"Anger and fear are feeling responses that occur automatically under stressful conditions. Her parents' judgmental messages about these intense feelings put Cindy into conflict with her own natural emotional reactions."**

Cindy had made a decision early in her childhood to be a perfect child. If she were perfect, then someone would really love and accept her *inner child.* Unconsciously, she left herself in an emotionally vulnerable position. When she was six or seven years old, she came to the conclusion that for her to be angry like her parents was bad. If she were angry like they were, she could not be perfect. Feeling angry is one of those flaws that keeps a person from becoming perfect. If she were perfect, cut off from her feelings, then she would feel safe in a volatile unpredictable world. So Cindy had to learn to cut off her emotions. She had to learn to numb herself or to bury her anger.

> **"Cindy had made a decision early in her childhood to be a perfect child. If she were perfect, then someone would really love and accept her *inner child.*"**

In this way, Cindy learned to be "nice," which, to her, is an important part of being perfect. Unwittingly, by distancing herself from her basic feeling responses to stress and criticism, she set up conditions under which her developing *Judge* could easily tap into the energy of her own feelings of fear and anger to keep itself inflated. She also distanced herself from her *inner child* who was so imperfect because she was sensitive and felt so much. By distancing herself from her own *inner child*, Cindy left it with no other choice, but to make a pact or a deal with the *Judge* in order to feel safe.

One essential condition of this deal with the *Judge* was that she had to be perfect — or else! Dire consequences would follow if she showed the slightest flaw. Her wounded *inner child* feels either grandiose or inferior. She does not know what it feels like to be an equal in a relationship with another person. Nor does she feel alive and spontaneous. She has given up her emotional life to keep her *Judge* from constantly intimidating and terrorizing her *inner child*. This is illustrated in the diagram on page 47.

"She also distanced herself from her *inner child* who was so imperfect because she was sensitive and felt so much. By distancing herself from her own *inner child*, Cindy left it with no other choice, but to make a pact or a deal with the *Judge* in order to feel safe."

The Calcium "Shell"

The wounded *inner child* in Cindy made an alliance with her *Judge* that, in order to feel safe, she would have to cut herself off from her own feelings by creating a "calcium shell." There is increasing clinical and research evidence that what Cindy learned to do with her feelings as a child actually produces a build up of excess calcium in her cells and tissues. This leads to what we refer to literally as a calcium shell. It became part of her emotional defense at the level of her cells and tissues. This further helps to block and numb her feelings. She doesn't even have to think about it anymore. It happens automatically because her calcium shell blocks and numbs her feelings.

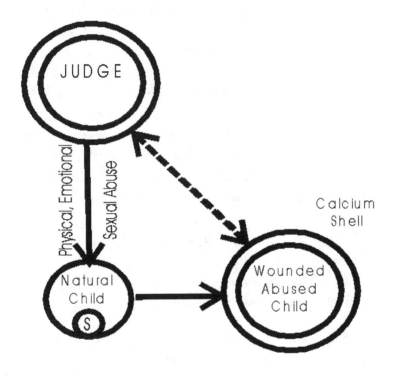

"S" is the spiritual core of the natural child. The separation takes place in response to any kind of abuse.

Other clients talk about having a wall that blocks their feelings and their relationships. We frequently see this calcium shell in a hair tissue mineral analysis that is done by a specialized type of laboratory. In this type of laboratory test, the calcium level is very high, especially in relation to magnesium. The high calcium level reflects a build up of excess calcium in the soft tissues of the body. This calcium shell develops out of the mind/body's need to protect itself from criticism, abuse, and unpredictable *Judge* attacks. It then serves as an additional psychological defense that operates constantly and automatically outside a person's awareness.

In the *Slow Metabolizer* who has an elevated level of calcium in the tissues, when magnesium is deficient relative to calcium, then a calcium shell will frequently form. This build up of a calcium shell is often the result of psychological stresses that keep the individual in a chronic "fight or flight" stress response. It appears that the mind will direct the body to build up a calcium shell that serves as a wall or protection against constantly feeling the chronic stress triggered by the *Judge*.

> **"It appears that the mind will direct the body to build up a calcium shell that serves as a wall or protection against constantly feeling the chronic stress triggered by the *Judge*."**

This phenomenon of a calcium shell is commonly seen in persons who are adult children of alcoholics (ACOA). The unpredictability of living with an alcoholic results in a mind-body reaction that produces a significant elevation of calcium in relation to magnesium. This process may also involve the loss of magnesium due to the chronic stress.

The resulting calcium shell serves as a mind-body defense against the awful feelings of fear, anger, vulnerability, and toxic shame that are commonly felt by children of alcoholics. The high calcium/ magnesium ratio associated with the calcium shell will also produce problems with blood sugar as well as problems with excess muscle tension and spasms. The resulting blood sugar problems will increase the person's risk for repeating the alcoholism and addiction patterns. Persons with a calcium "shell" will have great difficulty describing what they feel. They often say that they feel "numb," "dead," or they don't know what they feel. In such cases, a combination of vitamin and mineral supplements along with psychotherapy will lead to the breaking up of the calcium shell. When the shell breaks up, it is often described in the person's own words as a wall or a plate glass coming down or disintegrating. It may be experienced like a dam breaking and a flood of blocked feelings rushes in and overwhelms the person. When the calcium shell breaks up, an emotional crisis may occur because feelings are much more accessible to awareness and can be treated more effectively in psychotherapy. We have seen the breakup of our clients' calcium shell when they have defused the impact of their *Judge* and no longer need this additional psychological defense.

"...a combination of vitamin and mineral supplements along with psychotherapy will lead to the breaking up of the calcium shell."

The *Judge* and Survival

The *Judge* is very closely linked to survival issues for every one of us because the *Judge* develops in childhood around our stress response reactions to criticism, punishment, and abuse. The "fight or flight" reaction of the stress response is our basic survival response. Every time the *Judge* threatens the *inner child*, we experience an intense stress response. It is an automatic primitive mind-body reaction that bypasses our higher intellect. No matter how intelligent we are, no matter how many college degrees we have, no matter how many achievement awards we have earned, no matter how much money we have in the bank, we remain highly vulnerable to this intense stress response triggered by the *Judge's* threats to the *inner child.* This is why the *Judge* is so closely associated with survival issues — life and death. In fact, the *Judge* derives its psychological power by threatening the survival of the *inner child.*

The very nature of this reaction involves intense feelings of anger or fear. When we experience such an intense stress response, a great deal of energy is generated within us. Adrenalin is released and floods our body so that our energy increases. The *Judge* has no energy of its own. Remember, in adults, the *Judge* is only an illusion, a remnant of our early childhood traumatic experiences. Therefore, the *Judge* needs to draw energy from somewhere else, namely from the terror it stirs up in the *inner child.* This is why so many types of verbal or cognitive therapies are inherently limited in their effectiveness. The more the "fight or flight" response intensifies in response to a *Judge* attack on the *inner child*, the more our emotional reaction bypasses our verbal analysis and our intellect.

"This is why so many types of verbal or cognitive therapies are inherently limited in their effectiveness. The more the "fight or flight" response intensifies in response to a *Judge* attack on the *inner child*, the more our emotional reaction bypasses our verbal analysis and our intellect."

Ultimately, to be really effective in more permanently reducing a person's stress, a therapy process must be done on a feeling level to successfully defuse the power and control the *Judge* exercises over the *inner child.* For most people, this is usually accomplished by using a person's own imagery of the *Judge.* It is the image of the *Judge* deep within our psyche that overwhelms the *inner child.* When we can access that image and project it outside our psyche, we can see it for what it really is — a scary illusion — and we can deflate it like a big balloon. Then, we can really reclaim our own *inner child* more fully and completely. We will describe the therapy process in more detail later in Chapter 6.

CHAPTER 3

THE *JUDGE* IN DYSFUNCTIONAL FAMILIES

Pete was raised by his unmarried alcoholic mother and her assorted abusive boyfriends. His mother died when he was 12, but before she died, he often had to fend for himself just to survive. He remembers that when he was seven years old, he had to shop alone for groceries at the supermarket. When he was 11, he was in the car with his mother when she passed out drunk at the wheel. Pete had to scramble into the driver's seat and try to stop the car before they had an accident. These and other experiences contributed to his feelings of chronic stress, shame, and low self-esteem. He never felt quite good enough and he always questioned and doubted himself. Most of the time, when he wasn't anxious, he was depressed. He tried to keep himself busy so he would distract himself from these awful feelings. At an early age, he was labeled a "conduct disorder."

"The focus is just on survival, not on nurturance, optimal growth, and healthy development."

Some of the most lethal *Judges* develop in children growing up in extremely abusive and dysfunctional families. In such families, there is no communication. The focus is just on survival, not on nurturance and optimal growth and healthy development. In such families, they expect children to: 1) not disturb the alcoholic or mentally ill parent and 2) take over many adult tasks at too early an age because nobody else is capable. Then, if the parents act out anyway, they blame the child for being "bad" and causing the disturbance. In our workshops on the *Judge*, many stories are told by our clients about growing up in alcoholic and other types of dysfunctional families. Through their stories, it becomes clear how their parents' behavior and verbal messages laid the foundation for the development of the *Judge*.

Every child spends his or her earliest years in a family of some type, but many children also spend a great deal of time in other institutions such as day care or schools. The family, of course, is the major influence on a child's personality development. Johnny is fortunate enough to be born into a nurturing family. His parents care for him in a loving way and all is well with his psychological and social development. His parents' actions are predictable and consistent. He feels loving warmth and security. He feels safe and protected. He feels encouragement and self-confidence. However, in spite of all these positive experiences in his family, he will still develop a *Judge* component in his personality, but it will be small and most often, not a major problem for him in everyday life situations. Unfortunately, such families as Johnny's are rare in our society.

In dysfunctional families, the parents too frequently are *not* nurturing. Usually, the children have to take care of the parents for various reasons. The parents may be substance abusers, rageaholics, or mentally or physically disabled. Under these types of conditions, children usually feel much more insecure and anxious. Adult behavior is often unpredictable, inconsistent, and on many occasions, can be very threatening and scary. The adults will often be angry, critical, and harshly punitive in their treatment of their children. The children are under constant stress and feel like they live in a "war zone." They develop chronic stress and tension in their bodies. They never know what will happen to them next. With such constant stress and tension, the children will be ripe for developing an extremely harsh *Judge* in their personality.

"...in dysfunctional families the parent roles will be filled by individuals who are very undeveloped emotionally."

No matter the specific circumstances, in dysfunctional families the parent roles will be filled by individuals who are very undeveloped emotionally. That is, they will most often act out the parent roles from a child ego state rather than from a mature adult ego state. Or, in some families, an older sibling who really is a child does the parenting. This sibling is burdened with too great a responsibility. When parenting is done from a child ego state, there is a strong tendency for the child ego state "character" to rely on the *Judge* to try to establish control over the child or children in the family. This is usually done by threat, intimidation, punishment, and in extreme cases, by being abusive — emotionally, physically, or sexually.

The parent who relies on his or her *Judge* to impose control over the children also is operating from an insecure child ego state. In a such a child ego state, the parent will tend to operate either from a *grandiose child* place or from an *impotent child* place. In the case of the parent operating from a grandiose child place, the *Judge* will further inflate the grandiosity of the parent. In the case of the parent operating from an impotent child place, the *Judge* will serve as a mask to cover up the underlying feelings of fear and powerlessness.

In such dysfunctional families, parenting is inherently from a *Judge-dominated* position. That is, the *Judge* is the dominant part of the adult's personality. The adult is harshly critical and demands perfection from the children. Addictions of one kind or another are commonly found in such families. Since the parenting is coming from a *Judge-dominated* position, this will lead to constant criticism and will undermine the self-esteem of the children. This is what contributes to the prevalent low self-esteem of Adult Children of Alcoholics or Adult Children of Dysfunctional Families.

Children growing up in alcoholic and other types of dysfunctional families tend to have *Judge-dominated* personalities. The *Judge* in the personality of these individuals is the source of *internal* reinforcement of the low self-esteem which originally developed in the dysfunctional family. They were harshly criticized, punished, and sometimes severely abused. Nothing that they, as children, did was ever good enough for their parents. No matter how bright, talented, or motivated to excel the child was, it was never enough to satisfy them.

"They were harshly criticized, punished, and sometimes severely abused. Nothing that they, as children, did was ever good enough for their parents. No matter how bright, talented, or motivated to excel the child was, it was never enough to satisfy them."

In a dysfunctional family, not only does the *Judge* dominate the personality and behavior of the parents, but it also dominates the *entire family system*. The *Judge* becomes *institutionalized* in the dysfunctional family system and runs everybody's life. All of the members of such a family system tend to manifest strong personal *Judges* and these individual *Judges* reinforce the rules and dysfunctions within the entire family system. These family *Judges* also provide strong resistance to any attempts to cause change in the family's dysfunctional system. They do this by either enforcing silence about the dysfunctions and abuses taking place or excusing the dysfunctions and abuses. The *Judge* within each family member carries the rules and dogma of the family to legitimize the abuse and dysfunction as "normal" behavior. These family *Judges* give approval and act as if everything is OK. They provide excuses and explanations that enable the behavior to continue. The operation of the *Judge* within the personality of each family member and within the entire dysfunctional family system makes it very difficult to confront the important issues to change the system toward healthier functioning. Under such conditions, the *Judge* that is operating within such a family system would rather drive one of its members crazy or even to suicide than allow fundamental healthier changes in the dysfunctional system.

> **"Under such conditions, the *Judge* that is operating within such a family system would rather drive one of its members crazy or even to suicide than allow fundamental healthier changes in the dysfunctional system."**

The Natural Child and The *Inner Wounded Child*

A useful way to understand the origins of the *Judge* is to compare it to existing theories and to expand the concept. Transactional analysis (TA) theory which became popular in the 1960's sees the personality (ego) as divided into Parent, Adult, and Child parts. In a balanced personality, an individual has components of all three in their healthy aspects. The parent is the source of rules for living in society and transmits these rules while nurturing and protecting the child. The Adult is the information processor and is unemotional, like a computer. The child is the source of the emotions, creativity, and is connected to the Source of Being — the Life Source or Spirit. This is the ideal which can be diagramed as follows:

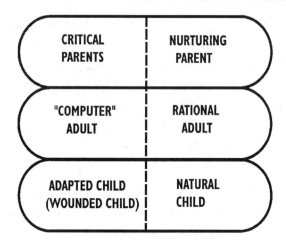

However, there are undesirable aspects to all the Ego states. The Parent can be critical, judgmental, and/or abusive, neglectful, or worse, and is usually called the Critical Parent in T.A. theory. The Adult can be *so* rational, logical, and computer-like that it's boring at best, and cold, uncaring, and cruel at worst. The child, trying to adapt to all the rules, demands, information, and circumstances of its life, may become the Adapted Child, constricting itself to fit into sometimes bizarre situations to survive. The diagram of this is seen on the next page.

Traditionally, TA has dealt with the "transactions" between people – how the Adult of one person might talk down to the Child of another, etc. This is useful, but we are using it to diagram the *intra*psychic relationship. That is, how the ego parts relate to each other and the difficulties that follow.

Expanding on the diagram, we see that the *Judge* is a pathological exaggeration of the Critical Parent (which may also be abusive or neglectful). It also has Adult and Child components *within* it. The Adult is super-rational and presents its rules as so logical that they can't be disputed. Whenever information becomes dogma, the *Judge* is operating. The Child part is very frightened, but has to keep the world from seeing this. It must keep others down and assert its power to feel OK. It may do this by having tantrums or rage attacks, or by quietly manipulating others.

Because the Natural Child (of the Ego diagram above) is so vulnerable and frightened of the power of the *Judge*, it will adapt to its rules and make an alliance with it to gain approval and to be spared its vengeful wrath. The Child may also identify with the *Judge* and reject the Natural Child part. The fundamental purpose of the *Judge* is to block the development of the Natural Child and, if necessary, to destroy it. We can diagram this as follows:

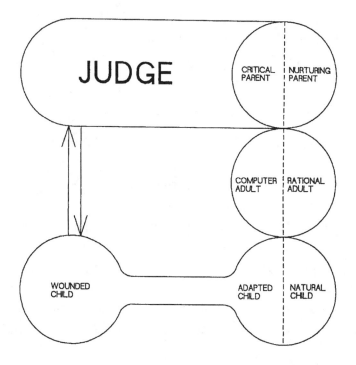

Two Personality Types

If the Adapted Child becomes very strongly allied with the *Judge*, it will overwhelm the Natural Child, giving it less and less space in which to grow in the personality. Because the Natural Child is the connection with one's spirituality, this connection may become more and more tenuous until the person becomes emotionally dead, empty, numb, uncaring, lacking meaning in life, atheistic, and without a purpose in life. The resulting *Judge*-dominated personality may come to look like this:

"J"-TYPE PERSONALITY

Or, in more nurturing families, the Natural Child may survive without being so crushed. The resulting Adult personality looks more like this:

"S"-TYPE PERSONALITY

This type of person has a *Judge* component in his or her personality, but it is relatively small and encapsulated. Generally, this component does not present so many psychological problems for the person. Compared with the "J" type, the "S"-type of personality is much easier to work with in counseling and therapy because such a person can more easily gain access to emotions. The "S"-type is much more emotionally alive, spontaneous, and creative. The bond between the *Judge* and the *inner child* may not be as strong in this personality type. It is easier to break the bond and free the *inner child* from the *Judge's* domination.

Usually, people with the "J" type of personality are much more difficult to work with in counseling and psychotherapy because their feelings are much less accessible. They have become experts at numbing and deadening their emotions. They also tend to intellectualize a great deal. These *Judge*-dominated individuals often don't recognize themselves as such because they think they are so "logical" and "reasonable." They live in their heads. They project their issues and behaviors onto the other person in the relationship. They resist working at a deep emotional level. They want to take a "problem solving" approach to dealing with emotional and relationship issues. When the controlling and judgmental behaviors of the "J" type of personality are confronted, therapy is often abruptly discontinued. Since therapy is basically a "mind game," some "J" type personalities may play along. If the process begins to challenge them on an emotional level or if it challenges their need to be in control, they feel threatened and they quickly terminate therapy.

There are two basic types of individuals with "J'-type personalities. One is much more obvious than the other. The first one is highly controlled and will usually be a stony faced grim serious person. The best question to ask of this type of person is, "When did you die (emotionally)?" These are emotionally cold, dead individuals who have lost touch with their bodies, their feelings, and anything natural or alive in themselves. They have no spark or spirit. Somewhere, sometime, someone snuffed the emotional life out of them. Or, sometimes, these individuals as children made a decision that the safest way to go through life is without feelings so that they don't feel emotional threat or pain. Early in life, they learn to cut themselves off from their body sensations and feelings. They learn to numb themselves. This also makes them very susceptible to drug and alcohol abuse. Chemical dependency helps them numb themselves and deaden their feelings. Nevertheless, substance abuse also loosens them up emotionally and gives them the illusion that they are enjoying themselves by "partying." The next morning when the hangover hits them, they realize what a price they pay for using substances to try to feel good about themselves.

"There are two basic types of individuals with 'J' type personalities. One is much more obvious than the other. The first one is highly controlled and usually will be a stony faced, grim, serious person."

The other form of the "J"-type of personality is the extremely controlling codependent who knows what is best for you and for everyone else. Their whole life is a struggle for power and control over everyone and everything. They can be very warm and friendly if they always get their way. They constantly intrude and cross other people's boundaries. They have a very grandiose *inner child* who constantly consults with the *Judge* to keep up-to-date on what exactly the other person should or should not be doing. These people don't make a move without consulting with the *Judge*. When you deal with this type of person, you will frequently feel drained and exhausted from the constant struggle with them for power and control. They never let up in this struggle. They wear you down.

The *Judge* has verbal, *pseudo*-rational "messages." It also has an emotional impact on the body, and the *Judge* has a visual image. The verbal messages, which often seem rational are really quite irrational when closely examined. They are similar to the "basic irrational ideas" of Rational Emotive Therapy. They represent dualistic thinking, i.e., either/or formulations:

EITHER	OR
I must be perfect	I'm terrible
Everyone must love me	I'm worthless
Everything must go as planned	It's a catastrophe
I must depend on someone stronger	I'm alone and abandoned
I must do all I can to help others	I'm a bad person
I must rescue others	I'm selfish
I must carry the burdens of others	I'm uncaring

In most cases, it is not enough to only address these messages at a cognitive level. In order to really change their impact on the body/mind (to have an emotional effect), one must work at the feeling level. This involves imagery (using all of the senses) and doing body work (massage, shiatsu, yoga, cranial sacral therapy, etc.) to release tensions and energy blocks which are held in the body.

The Impact of the *Judge* on Relationships

The *Judge* usually carries messages about how a relationship should be. Each of us learns about relationships from our perspective and experience as children. We come to some basic conclusions about male-female relationships as we watch our parents or others who are in close relationships. If we see love, respect, and caring, then these become a part of our messages and beliefs about relationships. However, if we see and hear yelling and screaming, physical abuse, anger and rage, coldness and emotional deadness, misery and unhappiness, then these too become part of our *Judge* messages on relationships.

When there are power and control issues within a relationship, there is usually a *Judge* at work being critical, manipulative, or abusive. The person operating from a *Judge* place will try to dominate the other person's *inner child* to gain control. This may be done by also tapping into the other person's *Judge* so that, in effect, there are two *Judges* attacking the *inner child.* The figure below illustrates this:

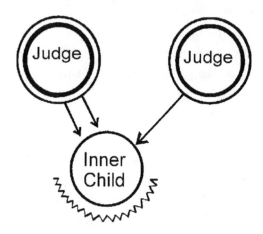

As this process continues, two possible directions will occur. One is domination by the *Judge* operating in one person and submission by the *inner child* in the other person. The *Judge* dominates and controls.

The other possibility is that the *Judge* operating in one person triggers a *Judge* reaction rather than an *inner child* reaction in the other person. Then the relationship has two *Judges* opposing each other with verbal attacks, accusations, and recriminations. Shouting, yelling, and screaming may intensify. The potential for physical violence escalates because the *Judges* completely take over the situation. Eventually, blind rage may break out, especially if alcohol or drugs are involved. The figure below illustrates this dynamic:

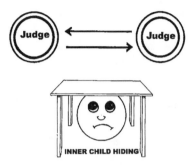

The *Judge,* operating outside people's awareness, may be considered a major factor in the breakdown of many relationships and our extremely high divorce rate. When a relationship does break down and divorce results, the intense feelings of hurt, fear, anger, and resentment set up ideal conditions for the *Judge* in both partners' personalities to become inflated and to take over the divorce proceedings. This is why it is so difficult for most people to have a friendly or amicable divorce. It is also why so many divorce proceedings turn out to be intensely adversarial and destructive emotionally and financially. Remember, the *Judge* always triggers survival issues associated with intense stress. The *inner child* in one or both of the persons feels that its very survival is literally at stake. This is why divorce is so often very painful emotionally and financially very costly. In our society, divorce brings out the very worst of the destructive impact of the *Judge* on people's lives. The power and control issues that came out in the relationship are then moved to the divorce court where they often become highly intensified by the *Judge* operating in each person. On a societal level, this same dynamic leads to the destructiveness of war.

CHAPTER 4

THE MIND-BODY CONNECTION: ANOTHER VIEW OF THE *JUDGE*

June is an attractive 33-year-old successful single career woman. She looks like she is in excellent physical condition, slim and shapely, but she does not feel well. She is in chronic pain from a lower back injury. She got this injury from over-exerting herself in aerobics classes. She also works long hours, mostly in a standing position. She does not sleep well because of chronic tension and back pain so she is usually tired during the day. However, she pushes herself to keep going because her achievement expectations for herself are high. She is a perfectionist. If she slows down, she feels guilty because she is not doing enough. She does not work hard enough. Her *Judge* tells her that she must look great and work harder to be the best or she is absolutely worthless.

June is an adult child of an alcoholic father and codependent mother, but she does not think that she needs to be in recovery or in psychotherapy. Her addiction is to perfection — a perfect appearance, a perfect boyfriend, a perfect job. Perfect, perfect, perfect! It's enough to drive her crazy because the slightest imperfection in her life is intolerable. She seeks all the right status symbols to convince herself that she is OK.

June's relationships with men always end in disappointment. Her career demands are leading her to workaholism that is adding to her pain. She finally reaches a point of both physical and emotional pain where she knows she has to change. She decides to try a yoga class.

"Her addiction is to perfection — a perfect appearance, a perfect boyfriend, a perfect job. It's enough to drive her crazy because the slightest imperfection in her life is intolerable. She seeks all the right status symbols to convince herself that she is OK."

June is used to stretching and bending in aerobics classes so she thinks she is in great physical shape. She thinks the yoga class will be easy for her, especially since the teacher and most of the students are in their 50s and 60s. Her *Judge* says, "They're old and probably are out of shape." As June struggles to do the yoga postures, the teacher encourages her to let go, not try so hard and allow herself to relax and to *breathe.*

June is amazed to find out that doing less results in effortless progress. She really doesn't have to work so hard and make it so difficult for herself. It feels good from the inside when she relaxes and lets go. It really doesn't matter what it looks like on the outside. She learns yoga is about "undoing" or "letting go" more than it is about achieving and reaching goals.

"...yoga is about 'undoing' or 'letting go' more than it is about achieving and reaching goals."

The more June lets go and relaxes, the better her back feels. Her sleep patterns also improve. She starts to lighten her work schedule and sees fewer clients each day. She begins to learn new ways to relate to her body. She starts to see it as part of a much greater whole rather than a "vehicle on the road to success." As she now says, "If your car breaks down, you can get a new one, but you've got only one body so you should respect it and love it if you want it to last."

**"...now she will be better able to use psycho-
therapy because she has already developed
some body awareness and some relaxing of
ego concerns."**

June has changed a great deal in a year of yoga classes. She is calmer
and has different priorities. As she has more time and energy for
relationships, she begins to see her destructive patterns. She is more
receptive to doing some *Judge*-work in psychotherapy. She needs to look
at her choice of either alcoholic men or anti-alcoholic perfectionistic men
who set off her own patterns of "addiction to perfection." However, now
she will be better able to use psychotherapy because she has already
developed some body awareness and some relaxing of ego concerns: looking
good on the outside and overachieving. Since the body/mind is one system,
it doesn't matter if we begin at the level of body or mind. Each affects
the other in profound ways.

Growing Beyond the Ego

The aim of most Western systems of psychotherapy is to <u>strengthen</u>
the ego, that rational integrating function of our minds that defines who
we are (different from others), what is our place in society and how to
"adjust" to that place in the best way possible. Never mind that society
may be irrational, *Judge*-dominated, limiting, and even stifling.
Paradoxically, in attempting to strengthen the ego by using only verbal
rational methods, many therapists may unwittingly strengthen the *Judge*
in the client's personality. This occurs when the *Judge* is provided with
new words and jargon, which it can use to give the illusion of psychological
change. This phenomenon is seen in many individuals who have been

in verbal therapy and know the language of therapy on an *intellectual* level, but have not made any significant change on an *emotional* level.

"...in attempting to strengthen the ego by using only verbal rational methods, many therapists may unwittingly strengthen the *Judge* in the client's personality."

Jacqueline Small is a transpersonal psychotherapist who developed a system of Integrative Breathwork for psychological and spiritual growth. In her book *Awakening in Time*, she speaks of "Adaptors and Transformers," those who adjust to the system and those who transcend it and work to change it. To transcend, one must move beyond ego. So, what is beyond the ego? How do we get there?

Two books that explain the relationship between yoga and psychotherapy can be meaningfully related to emotional problems and addiction recovery. One is *Yoga and Psychotherapy: the Evolution of Consciousness* by Swami Rama, Rudolph Ballentine, M.D., and Swami Ajaya, Ph.D. The other book is *Psychotherapy, East and West* by Swami Ajaya, Ph.D. Swami Ajaya is a psychologist who is American born and educated. However, as his Swami title suggests, he has also studied extensively with various sages of India. Swami Rama ordained him a monk.

The author of numerous books, Swami Rama was the founder of the Himalayan Institute of Yoga Science and Philosophy. He had extensive training in both Eastern and Western systems of psychology and philosophy, and has been a consultant to the Menninger Foundation in Topeka, Kansas. He also participated in many early experiments in biofeedback which showed how much the mind can control even the most automatic physiological processes in our bodies.

The information presented here on the Layers of Illusion is adapted from Swami Rama's books. The idea that the *Judge* resides at the level of mind (ego) and becomes a barrier to development beyond this level is our addition and reflects our own view. The philosophical system of Yoga, especially as explained in the books' *Yoga and Psychotherapy* and *Psychotherapy, East and West* can be meaningfully related to emotional problems and addiction recovery. The authors of these books speak of five "layers of illusion" that affect human consciousness. The outermost layer, obvious to all, is the body, a physical, mechanical entity that we can all see and feel. Medical science has looked at the body from a mechanistic viewpoint. Medicine attempts to treat illness in a mechanical way such as doing surgery on parts that don't work or cutting out and discarding diseased parts. This approach to human health is analogous to auto mechanics replacing worn-out or malfunctioning parts in a car. Such an approach to human health care is mechanical and "parts specific" as opposed to working toward healing the whole person.

"...we are made up of five "layers of *illusion*": body, breath/energy, mind/ego, wisdom, and bliss. Each layer seems real, just like the physical body, but each layer can be transcended to realize what is beyond it."

Hatha yoga also starts with the physical body, training it to be strong, flexible, and so forth. Many Americans are attracted to yoga for this reason. Yoga may create a more beautiful body, but it is much more than that and we are much more than that. The belief that we are only our body is an *illusion*. According to Yoga philosophy, we are made up of five "layers of *illusion*": body, breath/energy, mind/ego, wisdom, and bliss. Each layer seems real, just like the physical body, but each layer can be transcended to realize what is beyond it.

Transcending the body involves discipline of all one's physical habits — food, exercise, sleep, elimination, and sex. Not easily accomplished, it is a slow, gradual process outlined in the ancient system of yoga philosophy that is still relevant today. There are many good books available on the subject so we will not attempt to further elaborate. However, the other layers are transcended in the same manner, slowly, through patience, practice, understanding, and discipline.

Nutrition, sleep habits (physical processes) and working with the breath affects one's energy level. The breath is the connection between body, mind, and spirit. It is also the connection between voluntary control and the involuntary control of the autonomic nervous system.

"The breath is the connection between body, mind, and spirit. It is also the connection between voluntary control and the involuntary control of the autonomic nervous system."

The breath/energy level of existence is also the level of emotions. Children learn to block emotions and repress them by holding their breath and tensing muscles. Learning to control the breath can help you to release emotions when you want to and to control them when you want. Learning to use the breath helps to free you from being a victim of your own emotions and your *Judge*.

"Learning to use the breath helps to free you from being a victim of your own emotions and your *Judge*."

EXERCISE
for calming the mind, clearing anxiety

Lie on your back on the floor, body relaxed. Knees can be bent or straight, whichever is more comfortable. Put one hand, just below the rib cage, in the solar plexus area. As you inhale, let the area under your hand expand with the breath; as you exhale, let it fall back toward the floor. This is a passive movement, not forced. Let the breath be smooth (without pauses or jerks), even (your exhaled breath is as long as your inhaled breath), slow, and quiet. The breath gets longer and slower as you become more relaxed. Keep your attention on your breathing and don't let it wander off. Continue for a few minutes. Notice what has happened in your body and your mind because of this exercise. Stretch, roll to your left side and slowly get up. You can try this with or without relaxing music and see which is better for you.

This is just one example of the many breathing techniques available. Breathing can be used to relax, energize, release suppressed emotions of all kinds, and put one into altered states of consciousness as in Holotropic Breathwork. Many books have been written on the benefits of systematic breath work. A good reference on this subject is *The Science of Breath* by Swami Rama, R. Ballentine, M.D. & Alan Hymes, M.D.

"Breathing can be used to relax, energize, release suppressed emotions of all kinds, and put one into altered states of consciousness as in Holotropic Breathwork."

The next layer, more subtle than the breath and much more difficult to control than breath is the *mind*. The *mind* is immensely complex and is much more than its physical manifestation, the brain. Deepak Chopra, a well-known Ayurvedic physician, makes the analogy of the brain as a TV set. One can mistake the TV set for the whole phenomenon of television. In the same way, one can mistakenly believe that the brain is all of consciousness and when it is sleeping or "out of order" (diseased, intoxicated, or traumatized), consciousness ceases. The ancient yogis and rishis believed, and now modern quantum physics is rediscovering, that the *mind* is the individual expression of universal consciousness (present in every cell and molecule) and the brain is the physical expression of that universal consciousness. The *mind* has four states of consciousness according to the yogis: waking, sleeping, dreaming, and meditation.

"...the *mind* is the individual expression of universal consciousness (present in every cell and molecule) and the brain is the physical expression of that universal consciousness."

Our focus in this section will be on waking consciousness. In the waking consciousness state, the mind's functions are recording sensory impressions (perception), storing these as memories, forming concepts and forming an identity, a sense of "I am...," or an individual ego.

As infants grow, they begin to separate from the environment. They answer to their names. Their favorite words are "no!" and "mine," as their growing sense of autonomy expands. However, they are still dependent on adults to meet their physical needs and to provide security. The caretaking adults are much more powerful — they hold the power of life or death over small children. They believe that if they don't get adult approval, they may die. If their physical needs and emotions are shamed by the significant adults at this stage or, if they are physically or sexually abused, the ego becomes distorted. A basic sense of trust, safety, security and truth becomes damaged. Feelings of connectedness to the body and the universe are disrupted.

"If their physical needs and emotions are shamed by the significant adults at this stage or, if they are physically or sexually abused, the ego becomes distorted. A basic sense of trust, safety, security, and truth becomes damaged. Feelings of connectedness to the body and the universe are disrupted."

The child's sense of "I am ..." may become "I am worthless," "I am alone in a hostile universe," "I am unlovable." John Bradshaw has written a book *Healing the Shame that Binds You* on this phenomenon and another book *Homecoming* on healing through the developmental stages. These books are important contributions to our understanding of *toxic* guilt and shame that are feeling reactions to the impact of the *Judge*. The *Judge* is a formidable barrier at the level of the *mind* and ego. Until the *Judge* is confronted and defused (its power reduced), it is extremely difficult to move beyond this level of functioning.

By the time we are eight years old, the beliefs about who we are and what we must do to please others are very well developed. These beliefs form the cognitive components of the *Judge* and form the world view that we carry into adulthood. The emotional components become repressed. The original rage of the parent and the terror of the small child that formed these beliefs is pushed to the unconscious level. This usually occurs through breath-holding and muscular tension patterns in the body. We may act for the rest of our life as if we were following a "script" which says, for example, "I am worthless" and "I must be *super* competent to prove I'm not worthless."

"The original rage of the parent and the terror of the small child that formed these beliefs is pushed to the unconscious level."

All of the *Judge* messages form the basis of this "life script." Depending on how strong the messages are, they can be just mildly troubling or extremely destructive (a "tragic script") leading to addictions of all sorts, chronic pain, suicide or homicide. Since the *Judge* affects and is affected by the mind, breath, and body, transcending the Ego involves working on all three levels. Cognitive-behavioral therapy, which essentially works to change thought patterns, is generally not as effective for this work. For lasting emotional change to occur, it is necessary to do work with body, breath and imagery.

"For lasting emotional change to occur, it is necessary to do work with body, breath and imagery."

Mentally working to *quiet* the mind and all its chatter of "old tapes" (*Judge* messages) through meditation can be very helpful. It is in the quiet spaces between the thoughts that we glimpse the eternal and the spiritual, the higher levels of consciousness beyond the Ego.

We can also work cognitively on the level of waking consciousness with the *Judge* messages by beginning to question the assumptions, made when we were children, from the present adult perspective. Then we see that most of these assumptions no longer make sense.

We can work on the energy level by drawing or otherwise visualizing the *Judge*'s image (usually large and terrifying) from the child's perspective, gaining access to the painful or fearful emotions. Changing the breath and shifting body position, while guided by a therapist, helps us to become calmer, shift into a healthier, more adult aspect of ourselves and reexamine the fear and pain, and begin to let go of it. More will follow on these techniques in the chapter on treatment.

What about the physical level? Slow stretching with awareness, as in *Hatha Yoga*, makes us aware of chronic tension patterns that form our emotional armor and helps to release them. Releasing habitual tensions on the physical level opens new spaces on the *emotional* and *mental* levels — space for new ideas and healthier emotions. Working toward better nutrition, sleep and exercise habits gives us more energy to do this difficult work.

"Releasing habitual tensions on the physical level opens new spaces on the *emotional* and *mental* levels — space for new ideas and healthier emotions."

In summary, we can use body, breath, and mind techniques systematically to transcend that most troublesome part of the body-mind relationship, the *Judge*. The body is inherently "*Judge*-free" because it does not have the rigid concrete thinking and pseudo-logic of the *Judge* that resides in the mind as an illusion. The body is the source of our feelings, which are absent in the *Judge*. The body perceives, senses, and acquires information and data in a *Judge*-free manner, playing a key role in our *intuitive knowing*. Young children do this naturally.

"The body is inherently '*Judge*-free' because it does not have the rigid concrete thinking and pseudo-logic of the *Judge* that resides in the mind as an illusion."

In his book, *Entering the Sacred Mountain*, author David Cooper says:

"As long as people are unaware of the thought process, we are caught in the grip of a tenacious dragon called Mind. It often breathes fire, searing us in the heat of our own illusions, setting our blood boiling, but most importantly, causing us to believe that we live in a cave and that our job is to prevent anything from entering. The Mind dragon keeps us separated from the world.

The only way we can attain the wisdom teaching of kindness is to slay the dragon. How is this done? By realizing that this dragon thrives in the darkness of the cave, but cannot survive in the light. As we observe our own mental process, we bring a clear light to bear on the Mind-dragon, and sooner or later, it will melt away. And then, without additional effort, the lovingkindness within each of us will find clear expression because our essential nature dwells in the realm of compassion."
(p. 37)

If one works effectively on the body, breath, and mind levels, the ego gradually loses some power and the power of the *Judge* also diminishes. One experiences more times of inner peacefulness. One is less *competitive,* less interested in being "better than" another, less interested in worry, conflict and judgment. There are more times of spontaneity, creativity, and joy in life. One becomes more capable of even laughing at oneself and at life's eternal dilemmas, becoming more compassionate with others.

The Wisdom level includes much humor and a sense that "we're all in this together" rather than "every man for himself." There may even be flashes of great peace and joy, a strong feeling of being connected with a spiritual force and all of humanity. This is the transcendent or Bliss level at which powerful spiritual experiences are possible for anyone.

Below is a diagram of the 5 Layers of Illusion:

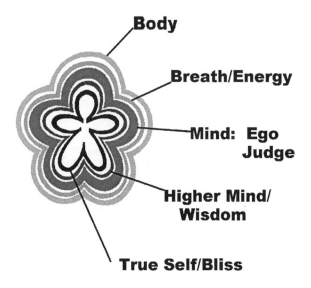

Body

Breath/Energy

Mind: Ego
Judge

Higher Mind/
Wisdom

True Self/Bliss

CHAPTER 5

JUNGIAN ARCHETYPES
AND THE *JUDGE*

In recent years, there has been a growing interest in the psychological theories and concepts of the great Swiss psychologist Carl Jung. A strong impetus to this trend was given with the publication of Robert Moore & Doug Gillette's book *King, Warrior, Magician, Lover* dealing with the archetypes of the mature masculine. Inborn psychological potentials are described by Jungians as archetypes or "primordial images." We believe that the formation and development of the *Judge* component in everyone's personality are related to these inborn archetypal qualities that Moore and Gillette so clearly described:

> "Jung and his successors have found that, on the level of the deep unconscious, the psyche of every person is grounded in what Jung called the 'collective unconscious' made up of instinctual patterns and energy configurations probably inherited genetically throughout the generations of our species. These archetypes provide the very foundations of our behaviors — our thinking, our feeling, and our characteristic human reactions. They are the image makers to which artists, poets and religious prophets are so close. Jung related them directly to the instincts in other animals." (p. 9)

In the context of the *Judge* and Jungian archetypes, one of the major characteristic human reactions is the basic stress response — "fight or flight." This is significant here because the *Judge* develops out of repeated stressful experiences with criticism, punishment, and, in extreme cases, traumatic abuse. The more negative a child's experience is with an inadequate parent who is emotionally underdeveloped, the more distorted and blocked will be the archetypal patterns. The *Judge* emerges later in personality development out of these negative stressful experiences and emotional blocks. Later in this chapter, you will see how this fits into the Jungian archetypes of the King, Warrior, Magician, and Lover.

> ## "The more negative a child's experience is with an inadequate parent who is emotionally underdeveloped, the more distorted and blocked will be the archetypal patterns."

Jungians also speak of archetypal *energy* potentials. A major function of the *Judge* is to block these natural energy potentials and to prevent their development into the higher mature forms of each archetype. In order for the *Judge* to maintain control over your life, it needs to block your development and maturation toward your highest potential. It resorts to all sorts of tricks and ploys to maintain its control. In each individual, the *Judge* selects certain weaknesses or flaws to exploit. The easiest ones for the *Judge* to exploit are the ones that are most easily measured — money, school grades, appearance, height, weight and so forth.

We frequently speak of having a *Judge* on some important aspect of our lives. Jim has a heavy *Judge* on his sexuality. His *Judge* triggers doubts about his potency and he feels highly anxious with sexual intimacy. At times, he may be impotent or, at other times, he may experience premature ejaculation in response to the intense anxiety he feels from his *Judge* on sexuality. Some of his *Judge* messages are that sex is dirty, sinful, evil, bad, or dangerous. He will face dire consequences if he has sex, let alone enjoys it. He may get sick or die.

"In order for the *Judge* to maintain control over your life, it needs to block your development and maturation toward your highest potential."

George feels a great deal of anger toward women and he believes that a sexual encounter is always a power struggle. He has to overpower and dominate women in order for him to feel safe and in control when he is with them. He also believes that women must be submissive to him.

Sandra has a heavy *Judge* on her money and on her financial security. With such a strong money Judge, there is no amount of money that will ever be sufficient to make her truly feel financially safe and secure. A feeling has always plagued her that there is never enough money to allow her to feel calm and satisfied. She always experiences an underlying feeling of deprivation and insatiability. This frequently leaves her with a feeling of being driven relentlessly with no time to rest. She may become a workaholic which is usually driven by an insatiable money *Judge*.

In these days of massive layoffs, company buyouts and mergers, the money *Judge* has many opportunities to become very active as stress levels go sky high. When the money *Judge* and the *Judge* on job security are so active, stress-related emotional and physical problems increase. If people have strong tendencies to resort to addictions to numb the unbearable feelings related to activation of the *Judge*, these addictions will also increase. These highly stressful economic conditions will challenge anyone's fundamental beliefs about financial security. Remember, when the money *Judge* is activated, no amount of money is ever enough to really give a person a sense of deep *emotional* security. No matter how much money a person actually has, the basic message of the money *Judge* is: "It's not enough. You need more, or else you will be destitute."

"...when the money *Judge* is activated, no amount of money is ever enough to really give a person a sense of deep *emotional* security."

The Four Jungian Archetypes

A person can have a heavy *Judge* on any one of the four Jungian archetypes — King, Warrior, Magician, Lover, or there can be a *Judge* on all four of the archetypes. The *Judge* originates out of the King archetype. It begins with the King, or the Queen in the case of females. The immature *shadow* sides of the King archetype are the *Weakling* and the *Tyrant*. The *Tyrant* King provides the origins of the *Judge*. At about eight or nine years of age, the *Tyrant* King is usually transformed into the *Judge* that splits off in the child's personality development and begins to operate as a separate personality entity. The *shadow* side of the King archetype is maintained by keeping the *Tyrant* King fully active, emotionally and behaviorally.

"The *Tyrant* King provides the origins of the *Judge*."

Moore and Gillette use a triangle model to describe each of the four archetypes and a pyramid to show their relationship to each other. A triangle represents each individual archetype. The top of the triangle represents the mature form of the archetype in its fullness. The base of the triangle represents the *shadow* form of the archetype. This *shadow* form reflects a bipolar dysfunctional psychological condition. The opposite poles of the *shadow* form of the archetype at the base of the triangle represent *active* and *passive* styles. From the perspective of the *Judge* concept, the opposite poles also reflect the polarized "either-or" type of thinking which characterizes the *Judge*. The *Judge* blocks their union and integration, thus preventing maturation of the personality. This is just one way in which we can apply the idea of the *Judge* to these particular Jungian archetypes and to explain how the *shadow* forms remain operative and dysfunctional.

"...the opposite poles also reflect the polarized 'either-or' type of thinking which characterizes the *Judge*. The *Judge* blocks their union and integration, thus preventing maturation of the personality... The *Judge* is the negative psychological force that maintains the polarity at the base of the triangle."

There is also another way in which the *Judge* can be applied to the pyramid-triangle model of these four archetypes. The *Judge* can operate at any level of any of the four triangular sides to distract or block growth and maturation. That is, the *Judge* can become activated to block a person's personality maturation at any level of development. The earlier the stage of development during which the *Judge* is activated, the more polarized the personality will be. The *shadow* side, with all of its dysfunctions, will be dominant. If the *Judge* becomes activated at later stages of personality development, then it will be operating at a higher level on the triangle so that personality development is not so extremely polarized.

We can easily apply the *Judge* concept to this pyramid model and its triangular sides. The *Judge* is the negative psychological force that maintains the polarity at the base of the triangle. It keeps the active and passive poles from coming together and integrating in a more mature balanced personality. This is illustrated in the diagram at the right.

As your personality strives to become ever more mature and integrated, the *Judge* will attempt to block and interfere with this natural growth process. It will attempt to prevent your personality from developing and maturing toward its full potential (moving up the side of the triangle). If the *Judge* is successful, the person's personality will be blocked at that particular level. Until the barrier of the *Judge* is removed, the person will feel stuck there at that level.

Since the model of the four archetypes is a pyramid, the *Judge* may be found operating at *different levels* on the various sides of the pyramid. For example, with a particular person, the *Judge* may be operating at the base level on the Lover side of the pyramid. Emotions and feelings will be extremely blocked and numb. On another side, the Warrior archetype may be more highly developed, but still be blocked. In this case, the *Judge* will be operating at a higher level on the triangle of the Warrior side of the pyramid. Overall, the *Judge* can be related to each of the four archetypes. Therefore, it can be found at some level on each side of the pyramid reflecting these archetypes. The example below illustrates how a person's *Warrior* aspect may be more maturely developed than is his *Lover* aspect:

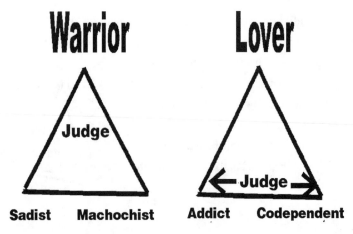

The *Warrior* Archetype and The *Judge*
—————— ∞∞〇∞∞ ——————

Rick first heard the *Warrior* archetype described at a men's conference in Tempe, Arizona a few years ago. John Lee, author of *The Flying Boy*, was the speaker. This Jungian archetype personally fascinated and intrigued Lee. It seemed to combine strength, commitment, spirituality, and the capacity for moral outrage. It had the power and resolve to set boundaries and limits in a fearless, firm, decisive manner. When John Lee described the *Warrior* archetype, not only did Rick hear the words in the *verbal* description, but, experientially, Rick felt the energy and decisive power of the *Warrior* in Lee's voice and body language. The energy and power of the *Warrior* came from a deep spiritual core. Rick knew immediately from an intuitive place that *Warrior* energy is ideally suited to confronting and deflating the illusionary power of the *Judge*. The *Judge* simply cannot stand up to *Warrior* energy. The *Judge* wilts and deflates like a balloon in the face of powerful and mature *Warrior* energy.

"The energy and power of the *Warrior* came from a deep spiritual core... *Warrior* energy is ideally suited to confronting and deflating the illusionary power of the *Judge*."

Shortly after Rick had heard about the *Warrior* archetype, he had an opportunity to hear Dr. Robert Moore discuss all four of the Jungian Archetypes described in his book *King, Warrior, Magician, Lover* (co-authored with Douglas Gillette). Rick was fascinated with Moore's descriptions of these archetypes because they embodied so many psychological characteristics that were easily related to his professional psychotherapeutic work. The *Judge* theory is at the core of this psychotherapeutic work.

"The mature *Warrior* is an idealized adult ego state that is in touch with the Higher Power and with Spiritual strength."

The *Judge* concept came out of transactional analysis and was related to psychological concepts of "ego states." From this original frame of reference, an "adult ego state" seemed to describe the best psychological place from which to confront and defuse the power of the *Judge*. However, since the *Judge* has such a profound psychological impact as to the intensity of the emotional response it triggers in a person, an "adult ego state" seemed too abstract and bland for dealing with the intense psychological impact of the *Judge*. The mature *Warrior* is an idealized adult ego state, which is in touch with the Higher Power and with Spiritual strength.

Warrior power and energy, drawn from the *Warrior*'s spiritual core, empower you to draw a firm boundary with the *Judge*. Since the *Judge* knows no boundaries and intimidates by threat, criticism, humil-iation, punishment and abuse, it is stopped cold in its tracks by the spiritually based power and energy of the *Warrior*. There simply is "no contest" because the *Judge* always operates psychologically from an immature parent, whereas true mature *Warrior* energy is strong, fo-cused and fearless.

"Since the *Judge* knows no boundaries and intimidates by threat, criticism, humiliation, punishment and abuse, it is stopped cold in its tracks by the spiritually based power and energy of the *Warrior*... The *Judge* always oper-ates psychologically from an immature parent, whereas true mature *Warrior* energy is strong, focused and fearless."

Over the past few years, we have found that many women will not be able to effectively relate to the *Warrior* archetype because they associate it so strongly with male aggressiveness and abuse. For many women, a strong spiritual feminine image will more effectively provide the emotional strength and energy needed to confront and deflate the *Judge* than will a *Warrior* image. We learned this while working with Sarah in a weekend intensive. We tell her story in the next chapter on Psychotherapy.

"Whenever a person operates psychologically from a *Judge* place, there is always a frightened uncertain wounded *inner child* present in the person."

Whenever a person operates psychologically from a *Judge* place, there is always a frightened, uncertain, wounded *inner child* present in the person. The *Judge* always serves as a mask and a cover for the person's frightened unsure wounded *inner child*. A close bond and alliance are between the *Judge* and the wounded *inner child*. Early in the person's development, the wounded *inner child* made a bargain with the *Judge* to feel safe and protected from constant threat, punishment, and abuse. A major part of this bargain and pact was that the wounded *inner child* must follow the life script that the *Judge* kept. The life script contained the expectations and limitations conveyed to the child by its parents on an unconscious level about how the child's life was to be. Any attempt to deviate from this life script would arouse the wrath of the *Judge*. This would be accompanied by terrifying threats of retribution and doom if the person did not immediately conform to these expectations and limits set by the life script.

"...terrifying threats of retribution and doom if the person did not immediately conform to these expectations and limits set by the life script."

A good example of how this pact is made and operates outside the person's awareness is shown in the following imagery. Jack's image of the *Judge* is seen and experienced in the form of a monster. He feels it is outside himself. He believes that his *inner child* is protected inside himself in a "dark cave" located in his belly. The pact made between his *Judge* and his *inner child* is that the monster *Judge* will remain outside if the *inner child* remains inside this dark, cold, confining cave. Any time the *inner child* attempts to leave the confines of this dark cave by opening up to light, feelings, creativity, spirituality, etc., the wrath of the *Judge* will be stirred. Depression, anxiety, guilt, and shame may be felt for no apparent conscious reason. The *Judge* has convinced the *inner child* that the safest place to live life emotionally and spiritually is in a dark, cold, confining cave.

When we can draw on our own *Warrior* energy, then it is possible to break free of the *Judge* and its tight control over our lives. Unfortunately, good *Warrior* energy is not found frequently in our culture. Therefore, good models of this vital energy are not readily available to our children and adolescents. One of the best examples of *Warrior* energy in recent times is found in Winston Churchill in World War II. The manner in which he rallied the British people carried a great deal of *Warrior* energy. Even in the darkest hours of World War II, when Hitler was fresh from his overwhelming victory over France, Churchill stood firm, determined to confront Hitler and the Nazis until they were completely defeated When you listen to his voice or see film of Churchill, not only can you hear his words, but you can feel his *Warrior* energy.

Now that we have described some theory and background concepts, in the next chapter, we will describe how these are applied in the therapy process to bring about deep emotional and behavioral changes. As you will see in the story of Sarah's Vase, not only does the therapy process require courage and determination on the part of the individual, but also a blending of maternalism and spirituality. You will also see the creative side of the therapy process in Kathleen's confrontation with her *Judge* whom her *inner child* called "Miss Shithead".

CHAPTER 6

THE *JUDGE* AND PSYCHOTHERAPY

After spending five years in psychotherapy and thousands of dollars, Mary felt very frustrated. She had worked hard to improve her life, and she had a good understanding empathetic therapist. They had talked for countless hours about Mary's problems. She had learned so much about how her early family experiences contributed to her depression and insecurity that it was clear to her why she constantly felt depressed and anxious. Intellectually she understood why she had such low self-esteem and so little self-confidence. If she now understood all of this, why did she still feel so depressed and anxious? Why did she still lack self-confidence? Now, after all this time in therapy, she began to think that she must be mentally ill. She must have something so terribly wrong with her emotionally that, even after spending thousands of dollars on five years of psychotherapy, she could not fix her basic emotional problems. Instead of feeling better about herself and her life, she actually felt worse. In fact, she began to feel hopeless and suicidal more often after therapy than she did before therapy. How did this happen to her?

"It gave Mary a lot of therapeutic information on a verbal level, but it did not have much effect on a deep emotional level."

When we view Mary's case from the perspective of the *Judge* con-cept, seeing what had happened is not difficult. She had worked primarily at an intellectual level in therapy. What she learned and became aware of had a great deal of truth and validity to it. It made a lot of sense. It was perfectly reasonable and logical. Unfortunately, this process did not have a substantial impact on her emotional blocks. It gave Mary a lot of therapeutic information on a verbal level, but it did not have much effect on a deep emotional level. In fact, in a very subtle way, outside the awareness of both Mary and her therapist, this verbal analytic process provided a great deal of evidence for Mary's *Judge* to tear her down and convince her of how sick and emotionally damaged she was. Throughout her therapy process, her *Judge* remained intact and unchallenged. It continued to have complete domination and control over her *inner child.*

> **"The purpose of *Judge*-work in psychotherapy is to help you to become aware of the presence of the *Judge* and its attempt to block emotional healing, recovery, spiritual growth, and creativity."**

The purpose of *Judge*-work in psychotherapy is to help you to beome aware of the presence of the *Judge* and its attempt to block emotional healing, recovery, spiritual growth, and creativity. It also blocks you from taking more personal responsibility for your own life and actions. It tries to convince you that you really can't be in control of your own life that there is something deep inside that really is in control. Of course, that something inside is the *Judge.*

As your awareness of the *Judge* increases, a confrontation ensues between the wounded *inner child,* the *Judge,* and our Adult ego state. The wounded *inner child* has been intimidated and abused by the *Judge* and continues to be emotionally affected by its psychological power. The *Judge's* frightening image and its threats seem very real to the wounded *inner child.* The Adult ego state part of your personality is capable of confronting and unmasking the *Judge.* This process deflates its intimidating controlling power. To the wounded *inner child,* the *Judge's* power is felt and experienced as frightfully real. The Adult ego state helps the frightened wounded *inner child* to see that the *Judge* is really an illusion — a terrifying memory from the past — that has no real power to terrorize and intimidate anymore in the present.

"The Adult ego state helps the frightened wounded *inner child* to see that the *Judge* is really an illusion — a terrifying memory from the past — that has no real power to terrorize and intimidate any more in the present."

Another way to describe what is involved in confronting and defusing the impact of the *Judge* is in terms of Jungian archetypes (see Chapter 5). Moore and Gillette describe four basic archetypes that operate in the psyche. In the present context, the mature *Warrior* archetype is a very powerful Adult ego state and is the most optimum psychological state from which to confront and defuse the *Judge.* Therefore, this archetype needs to be adequately developed in the individual in order for a successful confrontation with the *Judge* to occur. However, the word "warrior" applies much more to men than to women. Later, in this chapter, we will describe some powerful *Judge*-work done by a woman, not using a *Warrior* image, but, instead, using the imagery of a beautiful vase filled with golden white light. This is a very strong feminine and maternal image.

The energy of the *Warrior* artechype is very different from the energy of an angry child or adolescent. It combines strength, commitment, spirituality, and the capacity for moral outrage. It has the power and the resolve to set boundaries and limits in a fearless, firm, decisive manner. If you attempt to confront the *Judge* from the emotional state of an angry child or adolescent, such a confrontation will leave you in a chronic state of tension and stress, the "fight or flight" reaction. When you are feeling angry and tense, this negative emotional state tends to inflate the power of the *Judge.* This is a very important point to remember. As you learn to breathe and relax when the *Judge* is inflated, you will begin to notice that it loses its power.

"When you are feeling angry and tense, this negative emotional state tends to inflate the power of the *Judge.*"

The *Judge* is really an illusion psychologically and draws its power and energy from intimidating and abusing little children. It is a psychological "bully," having no real power or energy of its own. It is as if the *Judge* draws on the individual's own energy and stress to inflate itself. In contrast, the energy of the *Warrior* archetype is one of calmness, firmness, determination and strength.

The mature *Warrior* archetype is the strongest psychological state from which to confront the *Judge.* The mature *Warrior* archetype sets boundaries clearly and firmly, and is not afraid of being abandoned, rejected, or overwhelmed. Therefore, it cannot be intimidated by the *Judge's* threats or ploys. The mature *Warrior* knows that the *Judge* is an illusion of power and threats of doom. The mature *Warrior* holds its ground and the *Judge* fades in the face of the *Warrior's* calmness, aliveness, spontaneity and spiritual strength.

"The mature *Warrior* holds its ground and the *Judge* fades in the face of the *Warrior's* calmness, aliveness, spontaneity and spiritual strength."

When the *Judge*-work is completed in psychotherapy, the person experiences a wonderful sensation of relief and even a feeling of lightness and euphoria. This process of imaging, identifying, confronting, and defusing the illusionary power of the *Judge* is very empowering to a person, allowing creativity, spirituality, and self-esteem to develop much more fully with feelings of emotional freedom and inner peace. When the *Judge* has been confronted and defused, the wounded *inner child* can become more completely healed. It can grow more naturally and become better integrated into the adult personality, free of the stress and tension associated with being under the dominance of the *Judge*.

A major ploy of the *Judge* is to distract us from ourselves and to focus on "fixing" or "taking care" of another person with the message, "You should be responsible and take care of everybody else!" By confronting and defusing the *Judge*, your *Warrior* energy will become stronger and stronger. This will allow you to more effectively establish and maintain strong clear boundaries. Thus, this process of doing *Judge*-work in therapy can be highly effective in empowering you so that you can really make progress in recovery from codependency.

Therapeutic Setting

Our *Judge*-work is done with individuals, groups, couples, and in weekend intensives. In all these settings, we follow a general pattern of helping a person in identifying the *Judge* messages, creating an image of the Judge then confronting and defusing the impact of the *Judge* image or symbol. Creating the image is an essential part of this process. This is done primarily by using art and gestalt therapy techniques. We try to create an emotionally safe *Judge*-free atmosphere in which to do this work. Though we use a general model and approach, the therapy process is always unique for each individual participant.

Stories from a Weekend Intensive
on the *Judge* and the *Inner Child*
—————— ∞∞∞∞∞ ——————

These stories are composites of different people's therapeutic processes. There are so many common threads to the backgrounds of the people with whom we work. Typically, there is a history of alcoholism or drug abuse in the family background. Explosive anger and rage attacks on children are very common. Constant criticism, shaming, and humiliation are remembered by many of our clients. Physical, emotional, and sexual abuse have done extensive damage to these people's lives. Yet, it is often amazing how much inner emotional and spiritual strength remain within them, despite all the trauma they have experienced. It is really a tribute to the strength of the human spirit that it can survive and thrive as well as it does. Sarah's Vase is a wonderful symbol of this strength of the human spirit.

Sarah's Vase
—————— ∞∞∞∞∞ ——————

Sarah related a story of horrendous abuse by her stepfather that took place over many years. She was severely traumatized by repeated experiences of sexual and emotional abuse. Later, in her adult years, she had a nervous breakdown when she tried to do *inner child* work without being aware of the *Judge*. It was as if her *inner child* were brought back to the abuse and terror all over again without adequate emotional support to do this process therapeutically. She felt completely exposed and vulnerable with no one to turn to for protection. Psychiatric medications also did very little to alleviate her pain, anxiety, and depression.

Later, Sarah read a book that described the critic inside her that brought on some of her feelings of low self-esteem, depression, and anxiety. She was encouraged to embrace and to love this scary thing inside her. She tried very hard to embrace it and to love it, but her *inner child* was too afraid of it. The psychological reality was that her *inner child* really hated it because it was so terrifying, abusive, and controlling. She felt worse and worse about herself because the book had said that she should embrace and love this terrifying thing, but she couldn't bring herself to do it. She felt like a failure again because she couldn't do what the book said she should do — be positive and loving. It was like telling a child who has just been abused and terrorized, "You shouldn't be angry! You shouldn't be afraid!"

When Sarah was finally able to form an image of this thing that she was supposed to embrace and love, it turned out to be a horrible looking monster character with sharp teeth. The monster character sat on her right shoulder, constantly watching her every move and thought. It called all the shots and directed her life. No matter what she tried, it would not go away. It was determined to stay in control of her and torment her no matter what she tried to do.

Yet, despite all of her terrible abuse experiences, Sarah was still able to draw on a very powerful female image of strength and spirituality. The image and symbol of her female strength and spirituality was a beautiful vase filled with golden light. At first, she thought the vase was the part of her that shattered when she tried to do *inner child* work a few years earlier. Yet when she pictured it in her mind's eye, she noticed that the pieces had come together; she could see the form and the beauty of it. Much to her surprise, when she held the image of her vase in her mind's eye, lo and behold, the monster character on her shoulder shrunk down to the size of a small toad. She smiled with great relief. We noticed that the image of the vase had given her much more power and emotional strength.

"...despite all of her terrible abuse experiences, Sarah was still able to draw on a very powerful female image of strength and spirituality ... when she held the image of her vase in her mind's eye, lo and behold, the monster character on her shoulder shrunk down to the size of a small toad."

The next day, after Sarah had drawn a picture of the monster that sat on her right shoulder, she saw how closely it was connected to her sexual abuse experiences by her stepfather. The drawing had strong sexual imagery and sharp red teeth. It was really an awful image that brought up old feelings of stress and abuse. After she looked at it for a few minutes, she crumpled it up and threw it into a fire pit. She lit a match to it and watched it slowly burn up. She felt a great sense of relief when it turned to ashes.

Then, we encouraged Sarah to make a drawing of her beautiful vase on a large sheet of drawing paper. She carefully worked on the drawing on a picnic table. It was a warm summer day with a bright sun shining down on her near a shimmering blue lake. Her drawing was a beautiful crystal vase filled with golden light. It had a lovely curved form that was very feminine in appearance. It also had a flat base so that it could stand very solidly and firmly without wobbling. The vase filled the paper from top to bottom. When she held her drawing in front of her as she stood in the sunlight, it was as if the rays of the sun filled her vase with new light and energy. She absorbed the sun's warmth, light, and energy as she felt her own strength and power as a woman. Her face lit up and radiated with the warmth, light, and energy of her own drawing. She was able to make it a part of her.

This is a good example of how a woman can tap into her femininity and spirituality in the form of a powerful image to confront the *Judge.* Sarah's vase had the same power as the male *Warrior* to stand up to the *Judge* and deflate it.

The *Judge* in the Classroom: Miss "S"
———— ∞∞⊙⊙∞∞ ————

Kathleen is a teacher, author, artist, and Reiki master — a very successful and accomplished woman. Yet she still harbors some intense anger at her first grade teacher who discouraged her creativity almost from day one. Kathleen is very intelligent and visualizes easily.

We ask Kathleen to make a clay sculpt of her first grade teacher. She makes a very solid block-like clay piece about a foot high that looks very menacing with a long pointy nose. Rick asks her what this teacher's name was, but Kathleen doesn't remember. Then, when Rick suggests that maybe Kathleen's *inner child* knows, her six-year-old *inner child* gives a devilish grin and gleefully shouts, "Miss 'Shithead'!" We all break out in laughter as her description of this teacher's *Judge* starts on a humorous tone, though Kathleen's anger, fear, and pain are quite serious.

Kathleen then relates the following story. When her first grade teacher asked the children, "Who knows the alphabet?", a few could say it, but Kathleen knew how to sing it. The teacher punished her for this and ridiculed her for not saying it without the melody. This incident, added to the many criticisms and put-downs from her parents, squelched her self-esteem and creativity for many years. Her parents constantly judged and criticized her for being too creative and too sensitive.

"This incident, added to the many criticisms and put-downs from her parents, squelched her self-esteem and creativity for many years. Her parents constantly judged and criticized her for being too creative and too sensitive."

Here is Kathleen's clay sculpt image of her education
Judge whom she named "Miss Shithead." These are her
descriptions of the different sides of this sculpt. Viewed
from the front, "Miss S" has closed eyes that are "blind
to real children." She has saggy breasts that do not nurture

children. She has no arms with which to reach
out to children. Her creativity is balled up in a lump in her stomach
and is not available in her teaching. She has big heavy feet that
she uses to squash the spirit out of kids. As Kathleen picks up her clay sculpt,
we see that there is a little "squashed kid" underneath the feet of the teacher
sculpt. Everyone gasps as Kathleen shows us the child piece that is completely
flattened.

On the right side of Kathleen's sculpt, "Miss S" has a ruler
that she uses for measuring and judging children. This ruler
always measures them as "not good enough." The protrusion
from her mouth is like a penis that she uses to dominate vulnerable
children with her sharp criticisms and judgements.

From the back view of the sculpt, a snake slithers up her spine. This
snake whispers in "Miss S's" ear all the nasty things to say to
children. On the left side, where there should be a wellspring
of knowledge, "Miss S" keeps a vial of poison that she uses
to hurt children and to kill off their creativity and their feelings.

This clay figure of "Miss S" has a powerful emotional impact
on the group. Most people have had at least one repressive
judgemental teacher during their school years and can relate
to being judged unfairly and being put down by him or

her. The entire group, including us as co-leaders, gives a sigh
of relief when Kathleen removes the "squashed child" piece and
reshapes it into a star, holding it tenderly while she stands over
the "Miss S" figure to confront it from a stronger *Warrior* place.

As she looks down on this pathetic little figure, she realizes how impotent it is. However, she also realizes what a tragedy it is that such a pathetic figure be given so much power over vulnerable little children.

However, instead of using words to confront "Miss Shithead," she decides to take the clay piece out to the dock on the lakefront. She takes the sculpt apart piece by piece, throwing each piece into the water (since the clay is natural red clay, it is biodegradable). The group accompanies her and Sarah (who drew the vase in the previous description) brings her vase drawing as a female power symbol for Kathleen and as a shield for her own *inner child.* While singing the alphabet song, Kathleen takes apart her "Miss S" clay sculpt with much joy and relief. Thus, in this ritual she could reclaim her own creative powers and free her *inner child* from the destructive critical experience in first grade that had such a long-term destructive effect on her creativity and aliveness. For the rest of the weekend, Kathleen is more energized and enthusiastic. She has been relieved of a heavy psychological burden.

Stomping Out the *Judge*

The role of the *Judge* in psychological and emotional difficulties, codependence and addiction problems becomes quite evident when a person begins to draw the *inner child* and the critical punishing judgmental parent or other authority figure. Sometimes, a person may draw several *inner children.* Pat came from a very chaotic alcoholic home. She is a survivor of sexual and physical abuse with a strong tendency to dissociate when she becomes too stressed.

"The eyes are often an important feature of many drawings of the *Judge.* When children are being punished or abused, they often look at the eyes of the adult."

Pat's *Judge* drawing was of an abusive controlling mother with "crazy-looking" eyes. The eyes are often an important feature of many drawings of the *Judge*. When children are being punished or abused, they often look at the eyes of the adult. They become mesmerized by looking at the adult's eyes. They learn to go into a trance because the punishment or traumatic abuse feels so bad. Some drawings of the *Judge's* eyes show blazing rage. Other drawings show hollow eye sockets; it's like looking at a skull. Still others show squinting eyes shooting out sharp laser beams that cut to the soul.

When Pat holds her drawing up in front of her, it stirs fear and intense anxiety. She doesn't want to look at it — it's too scary. She recoils in fear. This is a very common reaction that people have in response to their drawing of the *Judge*. As they are initially making the drawing, the process begins to stir up intense feelings of fear and foreboding. It is as if they are opening a psychological Pandora's box that holds something very terrifying. There is an element of truth to this. Initially, the first conscious encounter with the *Judge's* image can be quite terrifying for many people. That's why it is best to do this work in a safe, supportive space.

After Pat holds the drawing for a while, then she can look at it and begin to talk back to it. However, she still hates the eyes. She feels extremely tense when she looks at them. Many people feel the eyes of the *Judge* are like laser beams that cut right through them. They feel totally vulnerable and helpless.

"When she covers the eyes with her feet, she no longer feels so frightened."

We suggest that Pat put the *Judge* drawing on the floor and step on the eyes. When she covers the eyes with her feet, she no longer feels so frightened. In fact, she feels more empowered and she also feels her anger.

We then encourage her to stomp on the face. She agrees to try. She does this with a great deal of energy until the entire drawing is in shreds (this is the defusing process). With a great sense of relief and a big smile on her face, she tears the remaining shreds into tiny pieces and throws them into the fireplace. She is visibly much more relaxed as she waits until the shreds catch fire. She watches them burn. Before this exercise, her feelings were flat and numb. However, after completing the exercise, she became much more alive and expressive. Like Pat, many women feel more power in their feet and legs. Using their feet and legs in this process mobilizes a great deal of energy and strength. Stomping on the drawing or clay sculpt of the *Judge* allows for a powerful venting of pain, rage, and terror that have accumulated over many years since childhood. It's important to find ways to vent the rage in safe ways that do not hurt yourself, others or destroy property.

"…many women feel more power in their feet and legs. Using their feet and legs in this process mobilizes a great deal of energy and strength."

A Demonic *Judge*

Fred, a very bright 19-year-old male student, is the oldest of two boys from a well-to-do family. His parents are divorced. He has been both physically and emotionally abused by his father since early childhood. His mother has been very passive, but emotionally over-involved in her style of relating to her older son whose *Judge* dominates his emotional life, his relationships, and his self-image. He has very low self-esteem, lacks self-confidence, frequently doubts himself, and experiences great anxiety whenever he has to make a decision.

Fred's drawing of his *Judge* shows a raging demonic male face that is grotesquely distorted. This devil-like image shoots lightening bolts and an electric charge depicts the impact of this abusive *Judge* on his helpless vulnerable *inner child*. Fred has such intense feelings of terror and panic triggered by this raging devil image of his father's *Judge* that his body shakes and his hands tremble whenever he feels judged or when he is in the presence of any strong authority figure. He has been so strongly conditioned to a male *Judge* attack that his body reacts on an instantaneous reflex level with panic and shakiness. In many ways, he has become much like his father, filled with anger and blind rage. He also is very impulsive and grandiose, with little sense or understanding of boundaries because his own have been violated in such intense and different ways by his father and his mother. We are very cautious about encouraging him to act out his angry feelings because his sense of boundaries and limits are so poorly developed

"It took a great deal of courage to stand up to this man and express himself so clearly. Fred felt greatly empowered and not nearly so afraid of his dad."

Fred says that his father "never listened to him," but we encourage him to write down what he would say if his father would listen to him. He declines and doesn't want to follow through on this suggestion. Still, several months later, he was able to have several confrontational discussions with his father about the childhood abuse he experienced.

Although his father was in denial about paternal abusive behavior, it was a major therapeutic step for this anxious young man to be able to confront his father. It took a great deal of courage to stand up to this man and express himself so clearly. Fred felt greatly empowered and not nearly so afraid of his dad.

Since Fred lives with his mother, he often places grandiose expectations and demands on his mother to give him whatever his whims desire. She has great difficulty setting limits on him so he often "wears her down." She frequently gives in to his wishes and indulges him. The women in the group give him feedback about how his grandiose demands and expectations might feel to his mother. Thus, Fred begins to get a sense of how difficult dealing with him has been for his mother when he is so impulsive and demanding.

Anxiety and the *Judge*

Another example of *Judge*-work was done by Marie. She has been married for many years, is the oldest of three girls, and is the designated rescuer of her elderly parents. She suffers from seasonal panic episodes that manifest as dizziness accompanied by intense anxiety. She is also a hypochondriac. Her symptoms are worse in the spring and summer.

Marie draws her *inner child* as "two" children — a natural child and an adapted child who is sad, lonely, and isolated. Her mother interferes with the joyful experiences of the natural child by being fearful, frequently asking, "What if...?" and saying, "You might get hurt," "Don't take risks," and so on. Her *Judge* is a humorous rascal who sits on her shoulder, saying "Ha! Ha! If you think this is bad, things will get even worse for you!" This type of gallows humor is seen in some *Judge* reactions. It intimidates and torments the *inner child*. She sees this image as "very strong and powerful." It has a strong hold over her.

"Her *Judge* is a humorous rascal who sits on her shoulder, saying 'Ha! Ha! If you think this is bad, things will get even worse for you!'"

As Marie looks up at the picture, she feels anger and strikes the picture, making a tear in the paper. It is a jagged tear, and she says it looks like a lightening bolt. The torn picture looks like this:

Marie realizes that there is less power now that the picture of the *Judge* is torn, but, as she says, she believes "it is still pretty strong." She tries to put the two pieces together and holds them with great effort. It takes awhile before she realizes that it is really she who has the power to hold this *Judge* image together. She believes it is her duty to keep it together no matter how much energy and effort it takes on her part, as she strains to hold the two pieces of the *Judge* picture together.

"It takes awhile before she realizes that it is really she who has the power to hold this *Judge* image together."

With some humor, we encourage her to hold the two pieces of paper together, then let them go and drop them. Sometimes, using humor in doing *Judge*-work helps to break the tension. This allowed Marie to move through the process more easily. Finally, she realizes that she has the choice of whether to hold her torn *Judge* together or to let it go. She can hold on or let go of being "mother's good responsible daughter" who listens obediently and absorbs all of her mother's fears. She has learned over the years to "carry" her mother's fears and anxieties as well as her own. Thus, she is very vulnerable to becoming overwhelmed by fear and panic. Letting go means asserting herself and setting limits with her mother. For the first time, she sees the challenge.

"...using humor in doing *Judge*-work helps to break the tension."

Donald is a man who has been separated from his wife for several months after his wife demanded that he leave. He is in the first stage of grief for the loss of his marriage, his children, and his home. During his visualization of the *inner child,* he saw two children — a sad helpless one and a hopeful, alive one under a rainbow. He saw his *Judge* as a crumbling wall (his life was "falling apart"). There were some holes already showing in the wall. We asked him to cut out the holes and to put the two pictures together. When he did this, he saw that the crumbling of his wall (the rigid world view of his *Judge*) could lead to new hope for his *inner child.* He cried when he saw this so clearly. Despite his intense grief over his losses, he was more alive and open with the group during the rest of the weekend. In this work, people often draw two *inner children* — one is a natural child and the other is an adapted wounded *inner child* who becomes closely bonded and allied with the *Judge*.

"When he did this, he saw that the crumbling of his wall (the rigid world view of his *Judge*) could lead to new hope for his *inner child*."

Another woman, Deborah, who is very creative and intelligent drew her *inner child* as a dark space under layers of isolation. Her family always thought she was "weird and selfish." *Judge* messages led her to hide and keep others away. The middle part is black and looks like a squashed heart. It also resembles an eye that watches her, waiting for her to do something wrong. When she looked at it, she felt fearful. We asked her to enlarge the *inner child* part. The second drawing showed an expansion of the heavy black heart. There was more space for her *inner child* to move about and there was a child-like form to it. On the outside, there was barbed wire to keep others out and to keep her gifts for herself, providing evidence to her *Judge* that she is, indeed, selfish. She generally doesn't trust others enough to come out from behind the wire, but will sometimes risk it. As she talks, she realizes that she is "coming out" in the group and doing that is safe. She is touched by the sensitivity and understanding she experiences from the group.

> **"As she talks, she realizes that she is 'coming out' in the group and doing that is safe. She is touched by the sensitivity and understanding she experiences from the group."**

Rebirthing the *Inner Child*

Helen is the youngest child in a large family. She is married and has two children of her own. She is a recovering alcoholic with several years of sobriety. She draws two *inner children*. One looks like a fetus and the messages associated with it are to be weak, translucent, quiet, and barely alive in a toxic womb. The other looks older, is very rigid, and is a *Judge*-like male. She sees this image as "stronger," but it doesn't experience emotions. We ask her to make the images in clay.

As Helen holds the clay images and defines them more, the fetus seems more warm and alive, and the flat "strong" dead child is not so strong as she thought. This flat clay piece begins to fall apart in her hand. She has to hold it very carefully in her hand because it really is very fragile, whereas the fetus fits perfectly in her other hand. It feels warm and alive and has a very natural, comfortable fit in her hand as if it really belongs to her. We ask her to pass these clay pieces around to each member of the group so they can also feel the difference between these two clay sculpts. The flat *Judge*-like child (whom she thought was so strong because its feelings were dead and numb) starts to fall apart. The clay sculpt of the fetus is truly solid and strong, but needs to be born again (at Helen's actual birth, she was unwanted).

We ask all of the women in the group to gather in a circle around Helen and to welcome her into the world. The men gather on the outside the women's circle. She cries and her knees shake as if she might fall. Each woman hugs her and welcomes her. She sits down feeling as if she has been reborn. The birthing ritual is a very moving experience for all of the participants. At the end of this process, many women are crying.

The *Judge* and Chronic Pain

Beth was referred through her counseling program at work because she had become so highly emotional, crying all the time, and feeling overwhelmed and depressed. She was taking Prozac for depression. She was also on other medications for her back pain and her other physical ailments

Beth made three drawings at home. One was a drawing of herself pushing a grocery cart down the aisle of the store when she was about 12 years old. At that time, a man in the store tried to molest her. Beth's father saw what was happening and came over and hit the man. Then, the father grabbed Beth and asked her what she did to "make the man do what he did." This is typical of a man's own anger inflating his *Judge* and accusing the victim (in this case, his own daughter) of making someone else victimize her. When they got home, her father banished her to her room, criticizing and shaming her for "what she did," furious with her and said it was all her fault.

The second drawing was of Beth's room to which her father banished her. This drawing reminded her of a dream in which she is in a rectangular closed swimming pool with the water rising higher and higher. She is terrified that she will drown when the water reaches the closed top. The third drawing was the "gestapo" supervisor who stood over her at work and made her feel so tense, especially in the neck and upper back. She had chronic tension in her neck, upper back, shoulders, and she had chronic headaches. When she looked at her drawing of the "gestapo" supervisor *Judge*, she instinctively recoiled in fear, tensing her neck, upper back, and shoulders. It looked like she became a frightened turtle pulling back into its shell.

"It looked like she became a frightened turtle pulling back into its shell."

As she worked on confronting this *Judge* image, the tension in her upper body released and she felt much more relaxed and "lighter." The following week, her chronic pain had decreased significantly. She also could not believe that her own simple drawings could have such a profound emotional and physical effect on her because, after all, she is "not an artist." As a result of doing therapy work on the *Judge*, many clients have experienced significant relief of chronic pain, tension, and even major shifts in physical illnesses.

What Becomes of the *Judge*?

When a person enters therapy and works on defusing the power and control the *Judge* has over one's life, what becomes of the *Judge*? Does it vanish or disappear? Does one ever become completely free of it? What happens psychologically and emotionally?

Until recently, it was never quite clear to Rick what happens when a person does *Judge*-work and reduces the impact of the *Judge* on one's life. For many years, he thought that he had very successfully reduced the impact and control that his own *Judge* had over him and his life. He was much calmer and far less "hyper" than he had been before doing this work. His blood pressure went from a mild hypertensive level to a normal level. In addition, he was far less codependent and felt much less need to control others.

However, recently, a personal experience added immensely to our understanding of what happens to inflate the *Judge* even after it has been largely defused through intensive therapy. One day, we were driving together to Northern Wisconsin to do a workshop, ironically, on the Judge and the Inner Child. We were running a little late so Rick's "time *Judge*" was activated and he was already tense and anxious about making good time. Being a Type A personality with a fast metabolism, he had a huge "time *Judge*."

Rosalie took over driving shortly before there was a major cutoff on the highway to get on the road to take us directly to our destination. Rick closed his eyes and took a short nap. An hour later, Rosalie awakened Rick to say that we were approaching the Tomah, Wisconsin exit. Though Rick was still half asleep, he knew immediately that we had gone in the wrong direction and we were at least an hour off the schedule. His anxiety and frustration immediately shifted into intense anger and rage. Both of us could feel his *Judge* inflate in an instant. It was an old familiar feeling to both of us and the "vibe" was awful to experience.

"His anxiety and frustration immediately shifted into intense anger and rage."

After Rick got out the road atlas and we found a route to get us back on track, he calmed down and reflect on what we had just experienced. It was really the first time that the whole process was so clear to Rick. Anxiety, frustration, anger and rage can instantaneously inflate a small dormant *Judge* into a full-blown *Judge*. It was an inescapable fact that it was Rick's frustration, anger and rage that triggered and inflated his *Judge*. He really had to own all of that and to do something about it. There was no doubt that the intense energy it took to inflate his *Judge* came from his own stress response. He realized that intense fear and/or anger and rage can provide the energy to inflate the *Judge* like a helium-filled balloon. He also wondered about where his *Judge* "hangs out" until it gets inflated again.

"…it was Rick's frustration, anger and rage that triggered and inflated his *Judge*. He really had to own all of that and to do something about it."

For most people, the *Judge* lies buried deep in the psyche outside awareness. The kind of intense threat and stress triggered by the *Judge* usually will not be felt as long as the person lives within the confines and restrictions of the life script. However, when the person begins to do something that is beyond the limits of the life script, the *Judge* is triggered and its presence is felt in a very intense way. Most people are not even aware it is the *Judge* that is making them feel so terrible. The *Judge* is most effectively in control of a person's life when it remains hidden deep within the psyche outside awareness. This is because it is psychologically an illusion with no real power of its own. Its energy and power come from our own stress response — our own fear or anger.

The illusion of the *Judge*'s power stems from its control and domination of the *inner child*. The tighter the bond and domination of the *Judge* over the *inner child*, the more the *Judge* dominates the person's life. Since Rick recently started to work with the Windows computer program, he has become familiar with "icons" in computer terminology. These icons provide a wonderful metaphor for understanding the process of *Judge*-work in therapy and in recovery.

Minimize the *Judge* to an Icon

The metaphor of the computer "icon" seems to fit the *Judge* phenomenon quite well and will make sense to many people who are familiar with this aspect of computer technology. It is as if you click the "mouse" when the arrow points to the *Judge* and you reduce or "minimize" it to the size of an "icon." Before you become aware of your *Judge*, it may loom very large psychologically and emotionally for you, but it is outside your awareness. This would be analogous to entirely filling the computer monitor screen with the *Judge* when you become stressed. There is hardly any space left for anything else — creative ideas, loving feelings, spirituality, etc. The *Judge* has taken over.

During the therapy process, when you draw or do a clay sculpt of the *Judge*, your psychological "computer screen" is entirely filled with the *Judge* image. As you are guided through the process of confronting and defusing the image and the emotional impact of the *Judge*, it shrinks in magnitude and size in much the same way as the image on the computer screen is reduced or "minimized" to the size of a very small icon. When the *Judge* is minimized in this manner, its impact also is greatly reduced. You feel tremendous relief and a significant reduction of an inner psychological source of stress. That is, the inner source of the "flight or fight" stress response is greatly reduced. The *Judge* then becomes like a very small computer icon in your psyche. By reducing the *Judge* in psychological size and intensity, a great deal more room is created in your psyche for love, creativity, and spirituality to emerge and develop.

"By reducing the *Judge* in psychological size and intensity, a great deal more room is created in your psyche for love, creativity, and spirituality to emerge and develop."

However, later, if you have an experience that is intense, frustrating or threatening, your stress reaction intensifies, and the psychological icon of the *Judge* is immediately enlarged or maximized. It instantly inflates in response to the infusion of the energy from intense fear or anger. Then you may be back in the grip of your *Judge*. However, with greater awareness and understanding, it will be much easier for you to recognize what has happened. Then, you can take action to calm yourself and, by doing so, you defuse the energy of the "flight or fight" stress response. This will shrink or minimize the size of the *Judge* again. This information and process give you the awareness and some effective techniques to begin to take control over this aspect of your life.

Gerald effectively used this metaphor to help himself defuse the overwhelming domination of his *Judge* over his life. In psychotherapy, he worked on his *Judge*, especially after he had a crisis involving an intense stress reaction at work, during which he thought he was having a heart attack. The paramedics were called and took him to the emergency room. Yet all of the medical tests and examinations were negative. Nothing physically was wrong with him. His symptoms were all stress related.

"What turned out to be highly beneficial to Gerald in therapy was for him to reduce his clay sculpt image of his *Judge* from a very large threatening angry face to a tiny icon — a miniature of the large terrifying *Judge* image."

In working on his *Judge*, Gerald made several drawings plus some clay sculpts of his father's raging judgmental face. Since Gerald worked extensively with computers on his job, he could relate to the computer metaphor of "icons" as they apply to the *Judge*. Icons are miniature symbols that represent different computer programs, such as word processing or graphics. What turned out to be highly beneficial to Gerald in therapy was for him to reduce his clay sculpt image of his *Judge* from a very large threatening angry face to a tiny icon — a miniature of the large terrifying *Judge* image. He smiled and was very pleased with his effort at minimizing his larger *Judge* image. He was amazed to discover that his psychological and physiological stress reaction to the smaller *Judge* icon clay sculpt was very different from his stress reaction to the larger image. With the icon, he was noticeably calmer and he felt much more in control of himself. With the larger image, he felt a significant increase in his stress reaction. He felt overwhelmed and out of control. He also discovered that, whenever he felt the *Judge* beginning to attack and dominate him under stressful external conditions, all he had to do was to picture the *Judge* icon and he would very quickly calm down. He was able to use his computer experience to enhance his therapy process greatly and to minimize the terrifying image of his *Judge*.

"...all he had to do was to picture the *Judge* icon and he would very quickly calm down."

Illustrated below is Gerald's clay image of his *Judge*:

Full size   Minimized to "icon"

A year later, Gerald had an opportunity to consider a job change and move to an area in which he had lived before, bringing him and his wife closer to both their families. He was able to weigh both personal and career issues very carefully and clearly. He also could resist *Judge*-dominated manipulations by his superiors and other executives who wanted him to stay in his present highly stressful job, although it no longer felt right for him.

What was so remarkable about this job relocation process for Gerald was that he could weigh the important issues in a very *Judge*-free manner so that he could decide for himself and his family as to overall quality of life issues. Gerald's experience with this process is a good example of *Judge*-work in psychotherapy and its positive carryover to new life situations and important decision making. He was able calmly and clearly to approach a critical decision in his personal life and career. He was aware of his "gut" feelings and could firmly act on them for the first time in his life, confident that no matter what happened with the job change and relocation, he and his family would be all right. By successfully reducing his *Judge* image to an icon size, he could take charge of his own life and career in a calm assertive manner.

"He could calmly and clearly approach a critical decision in his personal life and career."

This metaphor can also be useful in recognizing different types and degrees of *Judge*-dominated personalities. In common everyday experience, the two extremes of personality having a *Judge* component would be what we have called the "S" type of personality and the "J" type. The "S" type would have a highly reduced *Judge* component that would be more like the icon in computer terminology. It would be encapsulated — very small and dormant. There would be a great deal of room for healthy personality growth, emotionally and spiritually. Even without doing *Judge*-work in therapy, the "S" type person, under most conditions, just naturally has a small encapsulated *Judge*. In other words, it is usually always at the icon level so its energy impact is rarely felt except under severe stress conditions.

The "J" type of personality is heavily *Judge*-dominated. This would be like having the computer monitor screen completely filled with the *Judge*. It would usually be on "maximum" — very large, taking up most of the space. There would be little or no room for healthy emotional expression or spirituality. There would be more of a cold, threatening, unfeeling, uncaring quality to the personality. Such a "J" type personality tends to function like a robot, having a compulsion and drive for power over others. Underneath, deep within the psyche of the "J" type personality, there is a terrified, vulnerable, and powerless wounded *inner child* who also has intense rage. The *Judge* serves as a mask and a shield for this extremely vulnerable wounded *inner child.*

"...a 'J' type personality tends to function like a robot, having a compulsion and drive for power over others."

The "J"-type personality is highly resistant to doing any effective type of psychotherapy, especially a deep emotional process involving *Judge*-work. This is because the therapy process would challenge the extremely tight bond between the *inner child* and the *Judge.* In the "J"-type of personality, the *inner child* totally relies on the *Judge* for survival and protection, and cannot conceive of any other possible way to live other than total submission to the demands of the *Judge.*

This is one of the most common underlying psychological problems encountered when we attempt to do marital or family therapy. The strong alliance between the *inner child* and the *Judge* in one of the key family members results in sabotaging the whole process of change. Any situation or process that reduces the rigid protective shield of the *Judge* in the "J"-type personality is extremely threatening. Then, the extremely vulnerable wounded *inner child* would be completely exposed. This would be a terrifying experience for the "J"-type personality who is always into power and control issues in relationships. Ultimately, the *Judge* demands that others totally submit to his will. The ploys of the *Judge* are distraction, intimidation, and manipulation. It is always into power and control issues, with little or no capacity to deal with the "gray" areas of life between the extreme opposites. Everything in life is seen in terms of polarities — good/bad, right/wrong, black/white, us/them, me/you, and so forth. Also, for the "J"-type personality, nothing in life ever feels truly satisfying. There is always some deep unfilled void.

Can You Do *Judge*-Work Without a Therapist?

We believe that some people can do effective *Judge*-work on their own, but this depends on many factors. A primary factor is whether you are a "J"-type or an "S"-type personality. Overall, "S"-types do this process much more easily than "J"-types. "J"-types are usually so cut off from their feelings and are so much into their intellect that getting into this type of emotional processing is difficult for them. Another important question is whether you have a good support system. Is your support system *Judge*-dominated? Or is it more *Judge*-free? If your support system is not reasonably *Judge*-free, it typically will not be supportive of the emotional energy and courage it takes to confront and to defuse the *Judge*. This type of therapeutic work temporarily shakes up your basic personality system. Some very intense stress reactions may occur. For some people, these reactions may involve highly volatile and intense emotional responses. Intense fear, anger, and depression may be temporarily activated. It is like an emotional "detoxification" process. This is one major reason that our weekend groups have such a powerful effect for the participants. The safety and support that a person feels in a group as they are transcending their fears is quite phenomenal and it greatly helps move the process along.

After doing their basic *Judge*-work in individual or group therapy, or weekend intensives, many of our clients find that they are able to continue with much of the process on their own as the need arises. In their therapy process, they have learned the basic steps in the process and can draw on this knowledge outside a formal therapy session. This reflects the educational aspect of a good therapy process. Not only does it help to relieve stress, depression, anxiety and panic attacks, and low self-esteem, but what is learned in the therapy process is then incorporated into a person's overall life process. The knowledge and skills are applied in much the same manner as any other set of knowledge and skills are applied in day to day living.

The process of therapy and emotional growth is never quite done because life is a journey and the *Judge* is part of the human condition. Yet you will know when things are better for you. You will be more compassionate and forgiving with yourself and with others. You will have more emotional energy freed up from fear and anger; you'll be able to direct this new found energy towards loving yourself and others. You will feel an inner calmness, self-confidence, and self-esteem. You will notice that you'll spend more time in peaceful moods and much less time in the melodramas of life or "control dramas" as James Redfield, the author of the *Celestine Prophesy*, calls them. (See also the section on "What Becomes of the *Judge*?") You will find that you have more room and energy in your life to develop your spirituality and creativity. You'll feel a greater sense of connection to your Life Source. This is the hope and the promise of doing effective *Judge*-work. It is a profound life changing process.

"This is the hope and the promise of doing effective *Judge*-work. It is a profound life changing process."

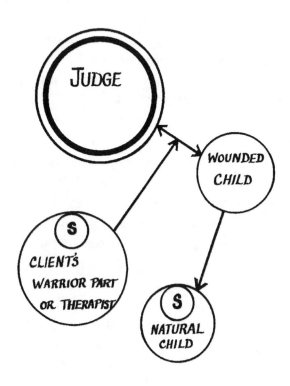

Part I: The Therapy Process:
Judge-Work

The *Warrior* part breaks the bond between the *Judge* and the wounded *inner child*, freeing it to reconnect with the *natural child* and be protected by the *Warrior*.

Part II: The Therapy Process: *Inner Child* Healing

As the *Warrior* confronts the *Judge*, the *Judge* shrinks or deflates, and the *Warrior* protects the *inner children* so they can integrate and grow. "S" represents spirit and aliveness.

CHAPTER 7

THE *JUDGE* IN RECOVERY:
ADDICTIONS AND CODEPENDENCE

Jack was desperate to stay sober and to make his recovery from alcoholism work. His life had nearly totally crashed. He had lost his driver's license after several arrests for drunken driving. He was thousands of dollars in debt and had missed many days of work because of hangovers from his drinking binges. His wife had grown tired of his constant drinking and divorced him. He knew he had to do something to sober up.

Jack went through a detox program and started AA. As he progressed in maintaining his sobriety from day to day and week to week, his mind started to clear. He read everything about alcoholism he could get his hands on and also listened to audio tapes on alcoholism and recovery. He was convinced that the more information he could absorb, the more successful he would be in his recovery. He wanted to work his recovery program in exactly the "right" way. After three months of sobriety, he thought that he now had a solid foundation of recovery. After all, he had learned so much in a short time and was following his AA program exactly the way he was supposed to, according to some "old-timers" in his AA group.

"He was convinced that the more information he could absorb, the more successful he would be in his recovery. He wanted to work his recovery program in exactly the 'right' way."

Much to Jack's surprise, the longer he remained sober, the more uneasy he became. At times, he became anxious for no apparent reason; at other times, he was depressed. For some reason, he began to question if he really was working his program exactly the way he was supposed to. He had been so sure that he was following it the right way. More and more he felt nagging doubts and the anxiety and depression seemed to be getting worse. He couldn't understand it. He had his drinking urges under control; he was sober; he was working very hard on his AA 12-step program — attending two or three AA meetings a week. Was he missing something? Was there something he wasn't doing that he should be doing? Before long, he found himself obsessing about his recovery program and his sobriety, as if something had completely taken him over. What could have happened to Jack during his recovery?

"Before long, he found himself obsessing about his recovery program and his sobriety, as if something had completely taken him over ... the longer he was sober and the more motivated he was to stay sober, the more his *Judge* was getting stirred up."

Jack couldn't understand why he started to feel worse after several months of sobriety and being so strongly motivated to work his recovery program. It didn't make any "logical" sense. However, from the perspective of the *Judge* concept, it made a lot of "psychological" sense. What Jack was not aware of was that the longer he was sober and the more motivated he was to stay sober, the more his *Judge* was getting stirred up. His *Judge* wanted him to drink and stay an alcoholic so that it could continue to maintain control over his life.

"Toxic Shame" and the *Judge* in Recovery

In his writings and lectures, author John Bradshaw introduced the idea that "toxic shame" is distinct from appropriate healthy guilt and shame. Toxic shame is the core emotional problem in addictions, codependency and destructive behaviors. We conceive of toxic shame as an emotional energy mass that differentiates into terror or rage. In 12-step recovery programs and in psychotherapy, some individuals seem unable to free themselves from the destructive effects of toxic shame in their lives. They may feel it as a heavy burden that weighs them down and brings on depression. Others may feel that they are exposed in a spotlight from which there is no escape; everyone can see them and see how bad they really are. With other people, the slightest frustration or criticism makes their toxic shame feel like a raw nerve or an inflamed abscess. This may then trigger rage or panic.

"We conceive of 'toxic shame' as an emotional energy mass that differentiates into terror or rage."

It seems clear to us that the concept of the *Judge* is closely related to what Bradshaw calls "toxic shame." The techniques we use in psychotherapy to help people identify, confront and defuse the emotional impact of the *Judge* would also be effective in reducing or eliminating their "toxic shame."

As we explained earlier, the *Judge* is an experiential psychological matrix that is formed by the summation of shaming experiences from infancy throughout childhood. After an accumulation of shaming experiences and other abuses (physical, emotional and/or sexual), the *Judge* matrix splits off as a separate psychological and emotional entity in a person's personality. When the *Judge* attacks the *inner child*, feelings of deep shame can be stirred.

> **"...any attempt to recover and heal from the effects of the alcoholic or dysfunctional family experience is likely to stir up the wrath of the *Judge*."**

Since the *Judge* is inherently an unhealthy anti-life and anti-spirit force in the personality, any attempt to recover and heal from the effects of the alcoholic or dysfunctional family experience is likely to stir up the wrath of the *Judge*. The recovery process can reactivate the *subjective* experience of the *Judge's* psychological impact. Feelings of fear, anxiety and vulnerability will appear and intensify for no apparent reason. The activation of the *Judge* is an attempt by this extremely unhealthy part of the personality to resist change and healing at all costs, even if it results in the recovering person becoming frightened, depressed and possibly suicidal. What Bradshaw refers to as toxic shame is among the basic feelings triggered by strong *Judge* reactions. The "should" and "should not" messages of codependency are essentially messages from the *Judge*. These have an intense emotional component as well as a verbal one.

Inasmuch as there is such a strong emotional part to the *Judge* messages of codependency, most recovering individuals will have great difficulty becoming free from the emotional control of their personal *Judge* simply by doing an intellectual and cognitive process. This may give them important information about their *Judge* messages, but it is rarely sufficient to release and change the *emotional* part.

> **"...emotionally and behaviorally, the person has succeeded in only becoming a 'dry drunk'."**

In addition to becoming aware of these *Judge* messages that are so damaging to self-esteem, most recovering individuals will need to identify and confront their *Judge* in a more intense therapeutic and healing process to defuse the emotional control and power that the *Judge* has over their lives. When this emotional and therapeutic process does not occur, then the individual may succeed in becoming "sober," but emotionally and behaviorally, the person has succeeded in only becoming a "dry drunk." Sobriety from the substance may be achieved, but the pattern of *Judge*-dominated alcoholic behavior and emotional reactions remain in place. The dysfunctional behavior and emotionality are driven by the *Judge* operating outside our awareness.

Many individuals can recover from their addiction or dysfunctional family experience by working a 12-step recovery program that includes a spiritual process. However, there are many other individuals who are so *Judge*-dominated that they are unable to continue their recovery without also doing the necessary therapeutic work. This involves learning to identify their personal *Judge* and to defuse its power over their lives. Until the *Judge* and its illusionary power are adequately defused and deflated, the recovery process for many people will remain blocked. They will become discouraged and at high risk for relapse.

As we saw in Jack's case, the *Judge* reacted as if its existence was threatened by his recovery and healing. The same process can occur in a 12-step recovery group. Some recovering individuals who are still dominated by the *Judge* (although they become sober) may feel threatened by recovery and healing in other individuals who are not so dominated and blocked. The one who is more *Judge*-dominated may try to intimidate other recovering individuals by collecting evidence that these other people are not "working their program," or that they are "in denial" when they are pursuing other positive activities in their healing and recovering process. "J"-type personalities (see Chapter 3) may convert the 12 steps into a dogma that they will interpret in a strict, rigid manner. This will lead to highly controlling codependent behavior in relation to other people in recovery.

In general, when a person follows the 12 steps in a rigid, mechanical, dogmatic manner, it is highly likely that the person is still dominated by the *Judge*. Remember, the *Judge* not only operates within the personalities of individuals, but it can also be institutionalized and dominate a system such as a dysfunctional family as we explained in Chapter 3. This has important implications for the addictions field and for those working with dysfunctional families and their members.

> ## "...when a person follows the 12 steps in a rigid, mechanical, dogmatic manner, then it is highly likely that the person is still dominated by the *Judge*."

When someone who has an addiction enters a 12-step program, there is a strong possibility that the *Judge* of this individual will begin to take subtle control over the recovery process. Recovery and sobriety may be permitted to go only so far before the *Judge*'s wrath gets stirred up and blocks any further recovery.

The *Judge* can operate in a subtle way. It is sometimes possible for a particular 12-step group to become dominated by the *Judges* of some of its individual members who claim to know the "right" way to recovery. Some may act as if they are direct descendants of Bill W. and have been handed the only road to recovery directly from him. Under these circumstances, a 12-step recovery group may become very *Judge*-dominated, outside the members' awareness. If this happens, then the group begins to operate more and more like a dysfunctional family and impedes the recovery of its members.

The *Judge* is a powerful personality entity that is found operating psychologically in virtually all alcoholic or other types of dysfunctional families. Therefore, it is important for those interested in the recovery process to become familiar with the characteristics of the *Judge* as well as how it can come to dominate not only the dysfunctional family. Sometimes it may also dominate the very 12-step group whose purpose it is to support the recovery of its own members.

For those of you who have made a commitment to your own recovery, a 12-step program may be necessary, but quite possibly not sufficient. It may also be necessary to enter counseling and psychotherapy to help identify and defuse the illusionary power of the *Judge* in order to remove a major psychological block to recovery.

Dealing with the *Judge* may be necessary to prevent a 12-step group from becoming *Judge*-dominated outside the awareness of its individual members. Individuals who work a 12-step program and also do their personal *Judge* work in psychotherapy are likely to have a much more rapid and effective recovery than individuals who only work a 12-step program. As the addictions and codependency field grows and expands, strong differences of opinion and even intense conflict are likely to develop as *Judge*-dominated recovering individuals feel threatened by new ideas and perspectives.

> **"Individuals who work a 12-step program and also do their personal *Judge* work in psychotherapy are likely to have a much more rapid and effective recovery than individuals who only work a 12-step program."**

Creative and innovative persons in these fields are likely to be attacked as *heretics* and traitors to the one "right" way to work a program and recover. Rigid individuals who are still dominated by their personal *Judges* may attempt to cite the 12-steps as "gospel" and use the terminology of the addictions and codependency field to unconsciously block positive change and development.

The concept of the *Judge* embodies both the cognitive and the emotional component of the destructive messages heard and experienced by Adult Children of Alcoholics and/or Dysfunctional Families. The deeper emotional work of confronting and defusing the emotional impact and control of the *Judge* then allows the individual to remove a major emotional block to recovery, healing, and spiritual growth.

The *Judge*, Spirituality and Recovery

An essential component of an addiction treatment and recovery program is the spirituality of the recovering person. Spirituality can be thought of and felt as a vital life force and energy. A crucial issue related to spirituality and life energy is discerning whether there are any emotional blocks or antagonists to it.

It is well known that low self-esteem is a characteristic common to virtually all codependents and addicted individuals. Contributing to low self-esteem is a large number of damaging critical judgmental messages and attitudes. These messages usually originate with parents, grandparents and other family members. Critical messages are often reinforced by dogmatic, cold, unfeeling and rigid teachers, clergymen, supervisors or other authority figures.

> **"Critical messages are often reinforced by dogmatic, cold, unfeeling and rigid teachers, clergymen, supervisors or other authority figures."**

What is not so well recognized is that these damaging critical messages and attitudes become incorporated into a personality matrix and are tightly bound with intense feelings of fear, panic, terror, worthlessness and vulnerability. As a child develops, this accumulation of critical messages and associated feelings of pain, terror and rage emerges as a distinct personality entity or matrix known simply as the *Judge*. The more dysfunctional the child's family is, the more devastating, overwhelming and intimidating the child's emerging *Judge* is likely to become.

The *Judge* is fundamentally an anti-life and anti-spirituality force, having deep emotional effects. The *Judge* is most clearly seen in the psychotherapy process, especially when visual imagery and art therapy techniques are used. Each person's *Judge* is uniquely and subjectively experienced at a deep emotional and physical level. Typical reactions to the activation of a person's *Judge* are either numbing and deadening of feelings or fear, panic and terror. These are the feelings that the child experienced when he or she was criticized, judged, punished or abused.

"Typical reactions to the activation of a person's *Judge* are either numbing and deadening of feelings, or fear, panic and terror."

In the psychotherapy and healing process (as we described in Chapter 6), when the client draws, or forms from clay, an image of his or her *Judge*, an intense emotional and physical reaction usually occurs. What is most important is the person's own emotional reaction to the *Judge* image. An objective observer looking at this same image would usually not be profoundly affected by it. This part of the therapy process helps to identify, objectify, confront and eventually defuse the power and control the *Judge* holds over the person's life.

The *Judge* knows no boundaries. It is extremely controlling and intrusive. Therefore, it usually plays a major role in codependence. Individuals who are dominated by the *Judge* most often tend to intrude on others and try to control them, most often from a place of grandiosity.

They "know" what is best for another person. A grandiose wounded "inner child" is behind such a *Judge*-dominated codependent approach.

Those who feel intimidated and victimized by the *Judge* allow themselves to be intruded on and to be controlled by others who are *Judge*-dominated persons. A victim of the *Judge* usually feels intense fear and resentment. The victim may try to fight back by manipulation, revenge or giving up and adopting a "poor me" position — the martyr position.

Others identify with the *Judge* and become the *Judge* in their attitudes and behavior. That is, they will act like an all-knowing and controlling *Judge*, attempting to control by intimidation, threat, intrusion and domination. They show an intense amount of anger and hostility, thus victimizing and abusing others until there is submission to their will. In his book, *The Celestine Prophesy*, James Redfield calls these types the *Intimidator* and the *Interrogator*.

Some people who are in 12-step recovery programs will be unconsciously blocked in their spiritual growth and development by the strong resistance — at a very deep emotional level — of their own *Judge*. It is in the nature of the *Judge* phenomenon that the more we develop our spirituality and create life changes, the more likely it is that the *Judge* becomes activated. We begin to feel vague fears, uneasiness, depression or numbness of feeling. In some cases, more intense feelings of vulnerability and suicidal depression are experienced. Such a reaction usually means that the wrath of the *Judge* has been stirred by our attempts to make significant positive life-enriching changes in the direction of spiritual growth, creativity and more aliveness of feelings.

"...the wrath of the *Judge* has been stirred by our attempts to make significant positive life-enriching changes in the direction of spiritual growth, creativity and more aliveness of feelings."

Therapeutic Issues in Working with the *Judge*:
Implications for Addiction Recovery

One of the most frustrating problems encountered in addiction counseling and psychotherapy has to do with clients' rejection of their own *inner child*. Some people in recovery or psychotherapy seem to have a great deal of difficulty accepting and nurturing their *inner child* and a heavy judgment is usually laid on this part of their personality. Whatever has happened to that child is its own fault; the *Judge* message is that the child "made" the adult do abusive and destructive things. One of the "deals" that the *inner child* makes with the *Judge* is to take full responsibility for the adult's abusive behavior and actions. This process can produce toxic shame and make the *inner child* feel unworthy of being loved, accepted, nurtured and healed. It also doesn't deserve to be protected from the wrath of the *Judge*.

> **"Whatever has happened to that child is its own fault; the *Judge* message is that the child 'made' the adult do abusive and destructive things."**

This unprotected position leaves individuals at high risk for relapse and/or a suicidal reaction. Feeling the impact of the *Judge* (especially outside awareness) is terrifying and unbearable. People adopt addictive and dysfunctional behaviors to deaden and numb feelings or to distract themselves from the impact of the *Judge*. When the *Judge* is active with all of its manipulations, ploys and threats, codependent behaviors become a major mechanism to distract us from our own shame, pain, impotence and vulnerable feelings. The *Judge* in the codependent says, "I know what's best for you, I'll take care of you, and if *you* change, then *I* will feel safe from my *Judge's* threats of disaster and doom."

We would like to suggest a model for understanding what may be occurring psychologically with people in recovery and what the counselor or therapist might do to help the person deal with the underlying issue. The *Judge* is the source of the abusive treatment of the child because the *Judge* part of the abusing adult person's personality despises and hates the aliveness of the *natural child.* Early in the abusive treatment, the adult's *Judge* attacks and traumatizes the *natural child* who has feelings, spontaneity, creativity, curiosity, intuition and a vital spirit. The *Judge* attempts to suppress and kill off the *natural child.* As the abuse of the *natural child* continues and intensifies, a part of the *natural child* splits off and becomes the *inner wounded child* of the adolescent and adult personality. (This is illustrated in Chapter 3.) The *inner wounded child* personality fragment is isolated and cut off emotionally and spiritually. Toxic shame, hurt, pain, terror and impotent rage are the primary emotions carried by the *inner wounded child.* Under such conditions, it is highly vulnerable to the threats, ploys and control of the developing *Judge*.

"The child becomes conditioned to living in a chronic state of 'fight or flight'."

The development of the *Judge* in the child's personality occurs with a great deal of tension and stress in the child's *body.* The child becomes conditioned to living in a chronic state of "fight or flight." On a physical cellular level, this wounded child personality fragment develops a "calcium shell" to block and deaden the terrifying feelings stirred up by the unpredictable violence and criticism of the alcoholic or abusive parent. The child becomes more and more numb to the ongoing trauma. On a psychological level, the *wounded inner child* believes that it has to submit and appease the *Judge* in the abusing adult's personality. The result is that the *wounded inner child* makes a bargain and an alliance with the *Judge* in order to feel safe.

The alliance that the *inner wounded child* makes with the *Judge* may have different qualities and conditions depending on the individual. In some individuals, the spirit of the *natural child* is so completely crushed that there is only an empty shell left. The resulting psychological vacuum is then filled by the *Judge*. (We described this process in more detail in Chapter 3 when we discussed the "J" type and "S" type personalities.)

When the "J" and "S" personality types come together in any group, especially in a 12-step recovery group, sooner or later, there will be clashes between them. The *Judge* of the "J"-type personality will try to intimidate and control the spirit of the "S" type persons. The "J" types adopt the 12 steps as their own "Bible" or dogma. They logically and reasonably make the 12 steps their own. As the aliveness and spirituality of the "S"-types grow, the "J" types become very threatened. In a grandiose judgmental manner, "J" types will tell the "S" types, "You are not working your program properly — the way in which it *should* be worked."

As the "S" types reach a point in recovery and personal growth where they need to move beyond the 12-step program, the "J" types may feel more and more threatened. They will often resort to judgmental manipulation and behavior to confuse and intimidate the "S" type individuals. If the "S" types are unaware that the "J" types exist in such a 12-step group, the "S" types may re-experience the childhood abuse by "J" type people again. They may give up their recovery and growth path, believing that they could never do it right anyway.

Psychologically, "J" type personalities are always emotionally operating from a child ego state since they are not emotionally developed much beyond 8 or 10 years old. Intellectually, they operate at a concrete, either/or level. One of our recovering clients describes "J" type persons as "graduates" of "Either/Or University." The school colors of this "University" are, of course, black and white. Behind the judgmental facade of the "J" type personality, there is always a hurt, terrified angry, vulnerable, and rejected *inner wounded child* with very low self-esteem. The function of the *Judge* in such a personality is to prevent anyone else from seeing this vulnerable part of the personality. The *Judge* uses all types of ploys to attack, intimidate, distract, and manipulate others in an attempt to appear "strong" and "in control." The *Judge* part of this personality type is usually prone to *grandiosity* on the one hand and *denial* on the other. In this context, codependent and addictive behaviors are fueled by the *Judge*. The Codependents tend to be grandiose in "knowing" what is best for others; addicts tend to be in denial about themselves and their addiction.

In psychotherapy, recognizing the difference between these two types of personalities is important for both therapists and clients. Psychologically, one main difference has to do with the nature of the alliance made by the *wounded inner child* with the *Judge*. "S" type personalities are usually quite capable of recognizing, accepting, and nurturing their *inner wounded child*. There is usually a weaker bond between the "S" type's *inner wounded child* and the *Judge* than is the case in the "J" type personality. For the "S" type, nurturing and healing the *wounded inner child* is easier and more effective once the encapsulated *Judge* has been identified and confronted from a strong *Warrior* position. Once this has been accomplished, nurturing and healing of the *inner wounded child* can readily be accomplished with love, caring, and intuition.

Inner child work with the "J" type personality is usually more difficult because the alliance and bond between the *inner wounded child* and the *Judge* is much closer and stronger. The *inner wounded child* is under the power and control of the *Judge* because there has been so much trauma and damage done to the child. The *Judge* in the "J" type personality dominates and rejects the *inner wounded child* as worthless and full of toxic shame. The *Judge* keeps reinforcing the message that all the abusive trauma and pain is the child's own fault — the child deserves all the misery it experiences. The *Judge* keeps reinforcing the impotency, shame, and worthlessness of the *inner wounded child* by blaming it for causing the abuse and trauma of childhood. This keeps the *inner wounded child* isolated, vulnerable, and desperately dependent. He or she most often turns to the *Judge* for "protection." The price of such protection is usually more abuse and humiliation. Thus, a vicious cycle is protracted and intensified. It is usually an excruciatingly slow, difficult process to drive a wedge between the *Judge* and the *inner wounded child* in the "J" type personality. However, until the *Judge* is identified, confronted and defused of its illusionary power, it is often extremely difficult for the individual adult client to effectively accept and nurture the *wounded inner child*.

> **"The *Judge* keeps reinforcing the message that all the abusive trauma and pain is the child's own fault — the child deserves all the misery it experiences."**

If the counselor or psychotherapist attempts to do *inner child* work prematurely with the "J" type of personality, a suicidal crisis may be precipitated. It is as if the *Judge* in this type of personality is determined not to give up power and control over the *inner wounded child*. A power struggle may ensue between the therapist and the client's *Judge*. On an emotional level, there is insufficient ego development in this personality type to wrest the *inner wounded child* from the power and control of the *Judge* easily. The *Judge* condemns the *inner wounded child* and utterly rejects it. This leaves the *inner wounded child* feeling totally isolated, abandoned, worthless, and doomed. Its toxic shame becomes too intense and terrifying to bear. It feels doomed and that the only way out is to die. Addictions develop in order to numb and deaden these awful feelings.

The task of the therapist is to support the client in identifying, confronting, and defusing the client's *Judge* before effective *inner child* work can be accomplished. The emotional strength of the therapist can help to drive a wedge between the client's *inner wounded child* and his or her *Judge*. The therapist can be a model of *Warrior* energy and behavior that the client can identify with as his or her own *Warrior* becomes stronger. As more and more space is created between the *inner wounded child* and the *Judge*, conditions become ripe for doing effective *"Judge-*work", i.e. imaging the *Judge* so that it can be objectified. This may be in the form of a drawing and/or a clay sculpt. Or, some individuals with an ability for strong mental imagery may simply be able to "see" the *Judge* in their mind's eye. For example, some individuals who read our articles or hear us talk about the *Judge* can immediately see the image of their *Judge*.

When the *Judge* has been imaged and objectified, then the therapist can help defuse its illusionary power and desensitize the client's *inner wounded child* from the threat and control of the *Judge*. In the presence of an emotionally strong and protective therapist, the *Judge* shrinks in psychological size, power, and intensity. There is an extraordinary type of energy and dynamic feeling that is subjectively felt by the client (to his or her amazement) when the process is done with awareness. (See Chapter 6 for examples.)

As the client's *Judge* is defused in power and intensity, then the healthier part of the client's personality, usually with the therapist's support, can reclaim the *inner wounded child* from the control of the *Judge*. From this point, more effective *inner child* healing work can take place. In our view, both psychotherapy and addiction recovery have this same process. This is a common link between the two fields. From the perspective of the *Judge* concept, one of the common problems in various types of verbal psychotherapy and counseling has to do with verbal information and analysis. Especially with a bright person who has a "J" type personality, verbal information and analysis may be taken in and given to the *Judge* in order to maintain even more effective control over the individual's life and relationships.

Without an awareness of the *Judge*, many therapists and counselors may unwittingly reinforce the dominance of the *Judge* in the client's personality by providing more and more information and "insight" into his or her problems. There are subtle ways in which therapeutic information and insight may be used by the *Judge* as evidence that the person is really "sick" or even hopeless. When the emotional and the body reactions are not substantially changed, the person may still remain stuck in old psychological and addiction patterns.

CHAPTER 8

THE *JUDGE* AND SEXUALITY

Since normal sexuality is strongly related to intense feelings of aliveness and the creation of new life, the *Judge*, of course, takes a strong position about it. Remember, the *Judge* is an anti-life, anti-spirit and anti-creation force. The *Judge* attempts to thwart any aliveness, feelings of spirituality or closeness and intimacy with another person. Finding flaws in our physical appearance and our appeal to the opposite sex is easy for the *Judge*. No matter how good we look, the *Judge* can find a flaw, however slight it might be. Sexual performance presents another opportunity for the *Judge* to have its say about our personal worth. Any self-doubt that we have about our sexuality can be exploited by the *Judge*.

> **"Finding flaws in our physical appearance and our appeal to the opposite sex is easy for the *Judge*."**

Another important factor that gives the *Judge* an opportunity to affect our sexuality concerns our intimate relationships. When we enter a relationship, we have some conscious needs we are seeking to satisfy but, outside our awareness, we are often attempting to find some nurturing for our *inner child*. Since our *inner child* is usually so dominated by the *Judge*, sooner or later in a relationship, we become vulnerable to a *Judge* attack. This may come from our partner or sometimes from our own *Judge* when we start to get something good for ourselves.

"...outside our awareness, we are often attempting to find some nurturing for our *inner child.*"

Male Sexuality

As Mark's fiftieth birthday was approaching, his wife, Barbara, and their children were all excited about their plans for a surprise birthday party to celebrate the big event. Yet, Mark wasn't feeling excited at all. He thought more and more about how old he was getting. He had more lines in his face. His hair was almost totally gray and he had a pretty good sized pot belly. He was not nearly as physically active as he used to be in his younger days when he played basketball, football and baseball. In fact, he was a very good athlete "in his day." However, now, he had all sorts of aches and pains in his joints and in his muscles. He was feeling old and "over the hill." Even his doctor was telling him that he ought to slow down and take it easy. After all, he was getting old.

The more Mark thought about it, the more he realized that he didn't have the sex drive that he used to have. Maybe it had to do more with Barbara getting heavier and less attractive than when they first got married. He wondered ever more about whether he still had any sex appeal to her. Without even realizing it, he found himself obsessing about his appearance and attractiveness to women. Maybe his doctor was right after all. He was getting old.

Mark noticed that he had much less energy and he began to feel depressed more often. He really is old and he could die suddenly at any moment. Outside Mark's awareness, his *Judge* was asserting itself and taking charge of his life again. This kind of life change, in this case, Mark's fiftieth birthday, provided fertile ground for his *Judge* to inflate and to become dominant in his life again. Before he knew it, Mark was flooded with self-doubts and worries about his health and stamina. He felt this uneasy feeling of doom hanging over him. The closer his fiftieth birthday came, the worse he felt. He began to experience more frequent outbreaks of anxiety and even panic for no apparent reason. Then, he would feel doomed and very depressed. He couldn't understand what was happening to him, but he felt more and more out of control. He was convinced that there was something terribly wrong with him — there had to be, otherwise, he wouldn't feel this bad.

In our culture (and many other patriarchal cultures), there is a very heavy *Judge* on male potency and sexual performance. The *Judge* is the ultimate scorekeeper and collector of evidence in life. Keeping "score" is common among adolescent and young adult males. "Scoring" sexually when he is with a female helps ward off the feelings of shame and humiliation heaped on a male by his own and the social *Judges* in his life. Not "scoring" is tantamount to being indicted and condemned by the *Judge* for being impotent.

One of the most common sex *Judges* is found in the *macho* syndrome. In this syndrome, the male presents himself as a strong "stud" who usually has a derogatory and contemptuous attitude toward females. The *Judge* in the *macho* male does not allow him to accept a female as an equal. However, deep down, he is a very frightened and needy little boy who doesn't understand female sexuality and is really afraid of it. Therefore he tries to control and dominate females at all costs. He often becomes very demanding sexually and feels that he is entitled to "get laid" because the female has "turned him on." Often, the male with this *macho* mentality also has a feeling of urgency about a sexual encounter since he will probably have a premature ejaculation that he can't control because of his underlying anxiety and doubts about himself. On the other hand, the other common male reaction to anxiety about sexual performance is to be unable to get an erection. If he does get an erection, he will quickly lose it due to his high anxiety and self-doubt.

The *Judge* in a male hides a terrified, insecure, anxious, confused and angry *inner child.* He is unsure of his own potency and personal power, needing to control and put women down. He is unconsciously in awe of the feminine mystique — fertility and power in the ability to conceive and carry a child and give birth. He is in awe of maternalism and all of its natural nurturing power, and yet, he is terrified of being cut off and abandoned by women.

The *Judge* in our culture fuels a great deal of competitiveness and aggressiveness in male children and adolescents. In fact, strength, competitiveness and aggressiveness are synonymous with masculinity, especially when sensitivity, warmth and empathy are denied. The latter are labeled by the *Judge* as *feminine* characteristics and therefore, according to the *Judge*, they are inherently signs of being "weak." Usually, one of the major attitudes of the *Judge* regarding the Strong-Weak polarity is that feeling and sensitivity are clearly signs of weakness and *not worthy* of a male and a "strong" person. This leads to a style of masculine behavior that focuses on creating a facade or a mask with external appearances of strength. The more *Judge*-dominated a young male is in our society, the more he must seek to prove his masculinity constantly, primarily sexually or aggressively. His *Judge* is relentless in its demands that he prove himself a man. This is particularly the case when our society does not have well-developed rituals and rites of passage for young boys to prove their masculinity in a socially acceptable manner and to be welcomed into the world of adult males.   The *Judge* plays a major role in exploiting the fears, suspicions and distrust that males and females have for each other. In this manner, the *Judge* in our society makes it very difficult to experience real intimacy and to express true feelings between males and females. As a collector of evidence, the *Judge* reinforces the attitudes, expectations and prejudices of one sex for the other. The *Judge* makes it very difficult for a person to feel truly safe with the person of the opposite sex because each distrusts the stereotypes of the other.

"... the *Judge* in our society makes it very difficult to experience real intimacy and to express true feelings between males and females."

One of the most common patterns of male/female relationships in our society has the male rescuing the "damsel in distress" or in need. The *Judge* will usually allow the male to play a magnanimous and generous role with a female as long as she is in such a weak and precarious position. This is because the male is "on top" when the female is in need. However, if his female partner becomes stronger, more independent and more spiritual, the male will often feel very threatened. His insecurity and fear will mobilize his *Judge* and it will try to block her growth and her increasing strength and independence. Most males don't know what to do with a strong independent female. In fact, most males are terribly threatened by such a development of strength and independence in a female. Rather than show his fear and vulnerability, the male will bring up his anger that will also inflate his *Judge* even more. This will escalate the power and control issues in the relationship. His *Judge* hopes to intimidate and overpower her *inner child*. His *Judge* hopes to regain control by getting her *inner child* to give in and submit to his will.

However, if the woman responds to the man's *Judge* attack by bringing out her own *Judge* to protect her *inner child,* the power struggle intensifies and escalates into an intense battle, usually with yelling and screaming. All kinds of accusations and criticisms are made by each. Under these conditions, with the two intimidating *Judges* fully activated, nothing can get resolved. Reasoning with a *Judge* is impossible. The relationship is headed for destruction unless one or the other can gain control from the *Judge* and give control over to the cooler-headed *Warrior* archetype.

The resulting anxiety, uncertainty and confusion found in a power struggle is fertile ground for the male's *Judge* to surface and to inflate even more. This leads to highly critical and controlling *Judge*-dominated male behavior. This is one of the most common scenarios in marriages and relationships in our culture. No matter how hard the woman works at pleasing her man, she will always fall short of his *Judge's* insatiable perfectionist demands and its need to be in control. The man's *Judge* will try even harder to intimidate her and to regain control over her. If these ploys don't succeed and she leaves him, his fear and anxiety will shift to anger and rage. The energy of this anger and rage may fuel his *Judge* even more. This often results in inflating his *Judge* to such huge proportions that his behavior is totally taken over by it, leading to more abusive and, sometimes, even murderous behavior. When a man is so completely overtaken by his *Judge,* he can go into a blind murderous rage. He doesn't see clearly, nor does he listen to reason when he is in this state. Extremely intense emotion takes him over completely. Paradoxically, this kind of intense emotion (fear, anger and jealousy) is not viewed by the male's *Judge* as overly sensitive and "weak." That is, this kind of intense male emotion is not viewed by the *Judge* in the same way that intense emotion is viewed in a female. The male's intense emotion is considered acceptable and natural. However, in a female, it is considered by the *Judge* to be weak and out of control.

From one generation to the next, the punitive or abusive behavior of the male is very closely associated with the *Judge* in the abuser's personality. A good example of this is in a recent article in *Changes* magazine describing the abusive and threatening behavior of the author's father. The author gives a classic description of her father turning into a full-blown *Judge* right after he has indulged himself and sexually abused her. He threatens her with the most dire consequences if she ever tells anyone about his abusive behavior and what he has done to her. She describes the icy cold threatening look in his blue eyes that are totally without feeling or caring. When a female child has experienced punishment or abuse by her father (or another male close to the family), her own *Judge*

will develop with its threatening, controlling messages, and an angry face
— either raging and overtly violent or stony cold and silent, but very
ominous.

> **"No matter how hard the woman works at**
> **pleasing her man, she will always fall short of**
> **his *Judge's* insatiable perfectionist demands**
> **and its need to be in control... When a man is**
> **so completely overtaken by his *Judge,* he can**
> **go into a blind murderous rage."**

Female Sexuality

A classic example of the *Judge* and femininity is seen in the movie
Snow White and the Seven Dwarfs. The wicked queen was obsessed
with her looks and had to be the "fairest of them all." The question she
posed in front of the mirror, "Mirror, mirror on the wall, who is fairest
of them all?" is a classic example of the *Judge* on female beauty.

The most powerful and destructive *Judge*
messages for females in our culture are on
appearance. The cosmetics and fashion
industries spend millions of dollars telling
women how they should look to be attractive,
desirable and beautiful. Women can do this
with the aid of the "right" products and
clothing to enhance their faces and bodies.
They are told they can *change* their faces and
bodies, not only with diet and exercise, but

with liposuction, plastic surgery, silicone breast implants, collagen
injections, *ad infinitum* or *ad absurdum.*

"The most powerful and destructive *Judge* messages for females in our culture are on appearance."

This *Judge* driven process erodes the internal personal power of women and makes them more dependent on *external* judgment. The more they depend on external sources to feel good about themselves, the more codependent they become. Losing touch with your own sense of personal power and well-being under such conditions is easy. Teenage girls and young women who have never developed a strong sense of themselves as human beings and as women have a great deal of difficulty developing a feeling of internal personal power with the constant bombardment of *Judge*-dominated messages from the media and advertising. All of the emphasis on outward appearance is not only very expensive and time consuming, but it absorbs a great deal of women's emotional and life energies. This is energy that could be used for "inner work" (personal growth) or that could be turned outward toward creative endeavors in the world of work or the arts, giving women more self-esteem through achievement.

In our society, little girls are given *Judge* messages from a very early age to:

> be nice (passive)
> smile, no matter how bad you feel
> be cute, attractive, perfect
> please others, take care of others before yourself
> not be too smart
> not be too aggressive (bitchy)
> not be too sexy
> don't enjoy your body
> not be too thin or too rich

find the "right man;" it's the key to happiness

find the "wrong man;" your love will fix him

These become the *Judge* messages that set up girls and women for passive dependent behavior that frequently keeps them victims of aggressive demanding males. The male side of this type of relationship involves a feeling of entitlement on the part of the male to have the female serve him sexually and emotionally on demand.

> **"*Judge* messages ... set up girls and women for passive dependent behavior that frequently keeps them victims of aggressive demanding males."**

If you are a female reader, look at the above message list again and be aware of how these affect your emotions and your self-esteem. List your own *Judge* messages or add to the ones above, garnered from your family, school experiences and your overall cultural upbringing.

These messages are at the basis of (1) many girls' dramatic drops in academic achievement as they reach adolescence and become more interested in attracting the attention of boys, (2) the very high incidence of eating disorders among young adult women and adolescent girls, followed by subsequent years of compulsive overeating, dieting, anorexia, bulimia, etc. and (3) the tendency for so many girls to become attracted to "bad" boys (those males who are violent, alcoholic, drug abusers and women haters) and to try to rescue them. Whole books have been written on each of these subjects, but what has been missing is a unifying underlying theory or explanation that focuses on the destructive basic *Judge* messages that drive the passive, codependent, victim behaviors.

Women are so deeply conditioned to smile and look cute that often, when they are trying to do anger work as part of the confrontation with their *Judge*, they will smile or giggle while saying angry words. Or they switch to helpless tears rather than getting in touch with appropriate *Warrior* (or Amazon) energy and outrage at what has been done to them. (See Chapter 6 for more detail on therapy.)

The *Judge* in Abortion

When an issue stirs intense feelings and passion on all sides such as with abortion, the *Judge* is often found at work. The intensity of the feelings and passion that many people have over the abortion issue fuels the emergence of the *Judge* in those involved. The presence of the *Judge* in the abortion issue is reinforced by theological and religious beliefs. These blend into cultural attitudes about women in general and about abortion in particular. Different families, especially alcoholic and dysfunctional families, may add to the intensity of the *Judge's* impact around the abortion issue.

Regardless of a woman's own religious or political views on abortion, there are certain realistic psychological and emotional reactions that are commonly experienced by most teen girls and women who have had an abortion. Among the emotional reactions is one involving very harsh *Judge*-based feelings. These feelings may include guilt, depression, anxiety and panic and suicidal urges. Often, they overpower the natural pain, loss and grief that are deeply felt. Also, outside *Judge* messages may further block the natural reactions. These outside messages may come from friends, relatives and professionals who attempt to minimize the psychological magnitude of the awesome decision to abort a pregnancy. "You shouldn't feel so bad about it." "It was the only thing to do." "What else could you have done?"

Sometimes, the very act of abortion is an attempt to hide the shame of the "dumbness" of the sexual act that led to the unwanted pregnancy. The *Judge* may already be at work in the agonizing process of making the decision to abort. Judgments about the "smartness" or "dumbness" of the person may be activated. Religious and cultural attitudes about female sexuality are often stirred up around abortion. The person's own *Judge* may accuse her of being a "whore" or a "slut," "evil" or a "murderer." *Judge*-dominated relatives, friends, or co-workers may add their own accusations.

Judge issues may arise at any place in the process of abortion — in the agonizing decision to have the abortion, during the abortion and afterwards. Feeling judged a "murderer" is not uncommon. As one woman succinctly said, "Many other female issues – abuse, rape, etc. – happen *to* you, making you a victim, but abortion is your own choice. It feels very different from any other female issue." Having made the choice and carrying it out means that it will never go away completely. Forgiving oneself and healing from abortion seems much more difficult than all of the other issues.

In working in therapy with women who have had an abortion, the intensity of the *Judge* is often extreme and it takes a great deal of work to really defuse its grip and destructiveness. It is as if the *Judge* thrives on the reality of the abortion as evidence that the woman is eternally damned. She can never really escape the reality of what she chose to do. It seems that the *Judge* can inflate this reality to block, demean, intimidate and torment the woman. The *Judge* can slyly use this event to inflate its own power and control over her life. Her essential worth and goodness as a human being is always in jeopardy.

In approaching the decision about an abortion, a woman is highly vulnerable to *Judges*, both internal and external. There is the pressure of the time *Judge* that makes it an urgent decision. The attitude of the man who impregnated her is a crucial factor. His fear or anger plays a big part in stirring up the *Judge*. Shame and secrecy also fuel the stirring of the *Judge* which may activate suicidal feelings. Social pressures increase, job and family pressures increase and financial issues arise which all test the relationship. All these stresses fuel the *Judge*. If alcohol or drugs have been used during the early stages of the pregnancy, this adds further complications to the situation. Will the baby survive and be healthy? Is it worth saving?

Since abortion is usually shrouded in secrecy, the woman is left to carry her burden alone. She is often urged to forget it and to get on with her life and no time or opportunity is allowed to experience the depth of her pain and grief. The return to normalcy, as if nothing really significant has occurred, is very common. The feelings become very deeply buried, but they fester like a deep, painful wound. It can become an emotional abscess because the *Judge* knows it is there. The *Judge* knows where to probe and to find it.

This emotional abscess has the potential to produce serious emotional or physical problems, especially when the *Judge* presses on it, bringing on painful or sick feelings. The *Judge* can make the woman feel that she deserves to be sick and in pain, fearful and uncomfortable. The *Judge* may make her feel panic or depressed and suicidal because she is made to feel that she deserves to die for what she did. The *Judge* shrieks, "What an evil, horrible person you are!"

> **"In our society and culture, the most malicious, malevolent and demeaning judgments about women and female sexuality are often stirred up over abortion."**

The guilt and shame associated with abortion often keep a woman isolated and alone in dealing with the agony and anguish of her abortion. Her self-esteem remains highly vulnerable to an attack by the *Judge*. The *Judge* holds on to the "evidence" of the abortion, ready to use it at anytime. Often, the *Judge* is an abusive male, but sometimes, it is female. In our society and culture, the most malicious, malevolent and demeaning judgments about women and female sexuality are often stirred up over abortion. This state of affairs makes it even more difficult for a woman to adequately deal with the emotional issues around her abortion. Healing and recovery usually require working with a *Judge*-free therapist in order to provide a safe environment. An understanding support group also can be very helpful. Using art to express the grief, the guilt and the shame associated with abortion can provide substantial relief and the first steps on a path of recovery.

The *Judge* and Menopause

If a woman's self-esteem is based on her appearance, menopause can be a very difficult time for her. The cultural "*Judge*-messages" tell her:

> you are getting old and useless
> you are no longer attractive
> you are drying up
> menopause is a terminal disease, the beginning of the end
> your body and mind are deteriorating

These can be very frightening and depressing messages for a woman if she believes that the *material* reality of her deteriorating body is the only reality and if she has not developed her consciousness of body/mind/spirit connections to be aware of the greater realities of her existence. Remember, the *Judge*'s function is to keep us blocked from developing our spirituality. The developmental challenge of menopause is to get beyond the earlier stages of form and function (which are both in the material realm) to a philosophy and sense of purpose (in the spiritual realm).

The medical establishment is quite willing to help women alleviate the "symptoms" of their "disease" called menopause. If you are a menopausal woman, you may get pressure to do HRT (hormone replacement therapy) for your hot flashes and dry vagina. Never mind if that puts you at greater risk for breast or uterine cancer. They can just cut these parts out because they are really just expendable organs. After your childbearing years, you really don't need them anymore. You may also get pushed to take supplemental calcium. Yet, if you take calcium, it can cause serious imbalances in your mineral patterns that may put you at risk for depression or panic and anxiety attacks. Still, they can "fix" that, too, with antidepressants (which make you more anxious) or tranquilizers (which can make you more depressed). Many menopausal women are at risk to become addicted to prescription drugs for mood alteration and pain control.

If you are disturbed about wrinkles and sagging skin, there is everything from wrinkle creams to face lifts for a small fee. Some of these treatments are useless, but others are painful and downright dangerous to your health. However, women continue to participate, driven by the *Judge,* in desperate attempts to keep their youthful appearance because of their fears of aging and losing their outward beauty. It is sad to see a 50 or 60-year-old woman who has had all the beauty treatments, dyed her hair, uses too much makeup, yet is still terribly unhappy with herself and increasingly unhealthy. Additional *Judge* messages that she should "try harder!" or "you haven't done enough" or "you deserve this!" only make her feel even worse.

When a woman does her own *Judge*-work in therapy, she begins to see that these messages are not permanently engraved in stone. There is more than one way to look at her situation. Dr. Deepak Chopra has written a book, *Ageless Body, Timeless Mind*, in which he states that aging is not inevitable, but is a result of your mental attitude. Obviously, the *Judge* plays a large part in our mental attitudes. Meanwhile, it is likely that most of us will have to continue to deal with our own aging process so let's do it gracefully with balance, harmony and self-love.

Some of Dr. Chopra's ideas come from Yoga philosophy, the same source of our ideas in the chapter on "Growing Beyond the Ego." Yoga philosophy views a person's life span in quarters. If you live 100 years, the first quarter should be spent learning the rules of your society and getting your education (developing your *Judge*?). The second quarter is spent working, gaining material possessions, raising children and training them (passing on the *Judge*?). The third quarter at 50 to 75 years should be spent learning who you really are (transcending the *Judge*) and blessing your children as they enter adulthood. The fourth quarter should be spent returning everything you have received in your lifetime: your material possessions and your wisdom so that you leave the world as you entered it, unattached and free to move onto a new state of consciousness — back to your source.

We think that this is a beautiful philosophy, one that makes "middle age" an exciting time of transcending the *Judge* and the Ego rather than a depressing time of physical deterioration. Doing the inner emotional work on the *Judge* and the physical discipline of keeping the body/mind healthy through holistic practices can make a great difference in the life process for many people.

Maternalism

A major area in which *Judge* messages adversely affect women is in their maternalism. From the time a woman becomes pregnant and her body changes drastically, the *Judge* on appearance is very active. If a woman's self-esteem is not solid before pregnancy, the flabby abdomen, stretch marks and lactating breasts can seriously challenge her feelings of self acceptance. Add in the exhaustion of new motherhood and you have a potent mixture for post-partum depression. It can be even more devastating if the pregnancy ends in miscarriage or abortion when there are issues of grief and/or guilt.

"From the time a woman becomes pregnant and her body changes drastically, the *Judge* on appearance is very active."

However, even after a healthy birth, nurturing a baby is hard if the mother has not learned to love and nurture herself. Accepting her body as a vehicle of nurturing is also very important for her (as in nursing). It is not just a sex object or something valued primarily for its appearance. If a woman is unable to accept the shift from *form* to *function*, she'll be unable to nurture the baby. Instead, she may set up power struggles or competition with the baby. Or she may withdraw from the scene altogether and leave the main work of raising the child to someone else: sitter, nanny, day care, grandmother or other relative. We realize economic necessity may be an issue here as well, but for purposes of this discussion, we want to look primarily at the emotionally loaded messages.

The *Judge* often has a field day with mothers, especially a new mother. Some common *Judge* messages around motherhood are:

> I'm not a good mother.
> I must be a better mother than my own mother was.
> I must be a perfect mother and have perfect children.
> I must be Supermom (working, raising children, having a neat home, doing community service and keep smiling).
> I must always be in control of my children; otherwise I am a failure as a mother.
> My children are an extension of myself (poor boundaries)
> If my children misbehave, it is my fault. Something is seriously wrong with me.

> If I don't want children, I'm selfish.
>
> If I want children, but can't get pregnant, then I'm a failure.
>
> If I have children and stay home to raise them, (according to some critics) I'm just lucky, OR (according to others) I'm lazy.
>
> If I go to work and put the children in day care (according to some critics) I'm ambitious, OR (according to others) I'm neglectful of the kids' needs.

The last four messages are "double bind" messages, meaning you can't win no matter what you do.

When there are marital problems or, if there is a divorce, the *Judge* may also become overbearing and dominate a young mother's thinking, feelings and behavior. She becomes highly vulnerable to the judgmental scrutiny of her husband or ex-husband. She can never be a perfect enough mom or do things right in raising her children. If she doesn't do things perfectly, he may have his lawyer "haul her into court" bringing her before a real judge. This will often inflate her own inner psychological *Judge*, substantially increasing her stress level.

"If they remain unconscious, outside your awareness, you are more likely to act them out on your children. That means that you become the *Judge*!"

If you are a mother, or are thinking of becoming a mother, look over these messages and consider their impact on your feelings and your stress. Which ones trigger your fear? anger? denial? helplessness? depression? What *Judge* messages could you add to the list that are especially meaningful to you? Taking some time to make these messages conscious reduces their destructive psychological impact. If they remain unconscious, outside your awareness, you are more likely to act them out on your children.

That means that you become the *Judge*! This happens when you feel overly stressed with anger or fear. These are the emotions that fuel the *Judge* and inflate it inside each of us. As you act on these messages, power struggles ensue. Your rage triggers terror in your child and the cycles of abuse continue. Abusive mothers have become stuck in an extreme Critical Parent/Rageaholic/*Judge* position. These mothers need outside intervention to help them get "unstuck." This usually means doing *Judge*-work and reclaiming their own *inner child.*

Look back at Chapter 3 on the *Judge* in Dysfunctional Families. This time, put yourself in the position of Critical Parent/*Judge* in the diagram. How does this feel? Remember, under every raging *Judge* is a vulnerable, terrified *inner wounded child.* By doing your own *Judge*-work, you will learn to free your own *inner wounded child* from the domination and control of your own *Judge.* Through the process of identifying, confronting and defusing your own *Judge* you will also free your own maternalism so that you respond to your children more naturally with good maternal intuition. This is one of the healthiest things you can do for the next generation.

There are several different approaches to teaching people parenting techniques. However, no parenting techniques will work well for long if a parent quickly falls back into a *Judge*-dominated place in parenting. The feelings and the "vibes" that come from the *Judge*-dominated parent will offset any good techniques of parenting. *Judge*-work is a powerful set of therapeutic techniques to change the underlying emotions that are often driven by stress. As stress builds up, it is easy for the *Judge* to become inflated by using the energy from one's own fight or flight stress response. Then, without even being aware of what has happened, you are acting from a place of *Judge*-domination in your parenting. It is extremely important for parents to become more aware of the stresses in their lives and to recognize how easily their own fear or anger brings out the *Judge* in them. They also need to communicate more openly about their own fear and anger to be more supportive of each other.

The Female *Judge*

The *Judge* in a female often hides a terrified, abused, anxious, angry *inner child* who has allied herself with the male *Judge*. She despises and feels contempt for the feminine in her mother who couldn't or wouldn't protect her from male judgment, punishment and abuse. There is a quality to the *Judge* in the female that can sometimes be more confusing and incongruous than the *Judge* in the male. Since maternalism is desperately needed for survival of the newborn infant and young child, a cold *Judge*-dominated mother figure is emotionally devastating because the child is so young, needy and vulnerable. Its very survival is tenuous. Negligence, physical abuse and punishment, rejection or abandonment all have a profound negative impact on the body and soul of the young child. This creates a "tissue issue" that is deeply felt. A tissue issue results from such early and severe trauma that it affects the child at a very deep body level — to the very cells and tissues. It is preverbal and, therefore, not helped very much by verbal cognitive talk therapies. Insight doesn't help very much with these emotionally deep pre-verbal problems — usually involving severe abuse that traumatically affects the child at a cell and tissue level. Art therapy can be very helpful in the healing of tissue issues. Many processes involved in art therapy are naturally healing, even without words being used to analyze the art productions.

CHAPTER 9

THE *JUDGE* IN HEALTH CARE

As Dick listened to the evening news, he began to feel more and more uncomfortable and a feeling of uneasiness and agitation began to come over him. The nightly news broadcast had one of its one minute health reports. Tonight's report was on diabetes and the importance of early detection. Diabetes ran in Dick's family health history. His grandfather had his foot amputated because of complications from diabetes and his aunt had lost her vision because of diabetes. Any discussion of diabetes had a really strong impact on Dick and this report had a serious ominous tone. It sounded like diabetes could be a silent creeping monster inside him that would suddenly overwhelm him when he was least ready for it. Then, he would be sick and crippled for the rest of his life. Just the thought of it disturbed him. After all, he was only 41 years old, watched his diet carefully, exercised regularly and had his blood sugar level checked every six months. Maybe he should have it checked more frequently just to be sure that diabetes wasn't sneaking up on him.

As Dick was growing up, his father sometimes commented about how cursed the family was with diabetes. It's in the genes. There's nothing that could be done to stop it. It's inevitable. Eventually it will get you. It won't kill you right away, but it will dominate your life like some monster inside you.

Now Dick noticed that he was feeling even more anxious and tense. What if he already had diabetes now and didn't even know it? If he waited another three or four months before he had his blood sugar checked, maybe he would pass out in a diabetic coma. What if it happened while he was driving on the expressway? He could get into an accident. He might be maimed for life or even killed in an accident. Dick could not shake off the increasing anxiety he felt. He was starting to panic. The ominous thoughts would not go away. At times, they seemed overwhelming to him. What had happened to him to bring on such tension and anxiety suddenly? Could it be a *Judge* attack?

In response to the news report on diabetes, Dick's *Judge* on health had been triggered. This *Judge* carried his father's fatalistic talk about diabetes in the family. It seemed as if nothing could be done to prevent this monster from taking over and dominating Dick. When he was a child, he often heard his father's depressing talk about diabetes in the family. It sounded very scary to Dick that it was in the family's genes and that the doctors would cut your leg off if you got it.

When Dick was listening to the news report on diabetes, his *Judge* overwhelmed his *inner child* with his dad's fatalistic message about how the disease ran in the family and how helpless everyone was to stop it. The *Judge* also warned Dick's *inner child* that they would cut off his leg if he ever got diabetes. This exchange between Dick's *Judge* and his *inner child* was going on totally outside his awareness. Even though the exchange took place outside his awareness, his mind and body both reacted to the threat of having his leg cut off. He panicked without even being aware of what it really was all about. He could not control his own intense anxiety reaction because he had no idea what was really going on deep within his psyche.

As John prepared to leave his house for the doctor's office to get his annual physical checkup, he noticed that he was feeling more tense than usual. His palms were sweaty and his heart was racing and pounding for no apparent reason. He stopped for a moment to ponder his unusually tense reaction, but he couldn't come up with anything. Everything seemed to be going well in his life. He had a good job and was earning a comfortable salary with a nice bonus at the end of each year. He always got good reviews of his job performance. He had a good relationship with his girlfriend, Joan. They had been going together for the past four years and were very comfortable with each other. John also thought about what good shape he was in for a young man of 29. He regularly worked out at the health club three times a week and his body fat percentage was low. He liked the well-toned muscles of his body — they showed good definition and Joan also seemed to like that. He liked his bright red sports car with all the extras and his luxurious condo on a golf course. John had achieved much more in life at this stage than his father had achieved in a lifetime of hard work. Nevertheless, there were also fleeting thoughts about what the doctor might discover about him. Maybe something was going on inside him that he wasn't even aware of, the start of some major illness.

As John settled comfortably into the soft leather seat of his sports car to drive to the doctor's office, he began to feel more and more uneasy. It was only a short drive to the doctor's, but the closer he got to the clinic, the more nervous and anxious he became. His heart was really pounding and the sweat on the leather steering wheel made it feel slippery and harder to hold on to. It was making him worry about losing control of the slippery steering wheel. What if he lost control and got into a serious accident? He tightened his grip on the steering wheel. But, the tighter he held on, the more slippery it felt. He really began to feel anxious and knew he was becoming more and more tense. Sweat started to bead on his forehead and he felt cold and clammy. Now he was feeling totally panicked and out of control. He became so preoccupied with what was happening to him that he lost focus on the traffic around him. Then he glanced in the mirror and saw the car behind him. He felt pressured and pushed to go faster. He wasn't going fast enough and the driver behind him was getting impatient and angry with him. What was the matter with him? Didn't he know how to drive in traffic? John suddenly hit the brakes and brought his car to a panic stop. He was shaking and frozen in fear. He had almost caused an accident. What had happened to John?

John had started out feeling fine. However, as he got more focused on going to the doctor's office for his routine annual physical exam, he had begun to feel uneasy. This uneasy feeling intensified and turned into a full-blown panic attack. He had always been so stable and so much in control. Now, here he was, an emotional mess, feeling totally panicked and out of control.

John had just experienced a *Judge* attack. Somewhere, deep inside his psyche, his *Judge* had inflated like a huge balloon with a scary, angry face on it. The eyes were narrowed into thin slits with an icy cold glare that felt like penetrating laser beams. The *Judge* was furious with John. How dare he be so smug and self-satisfied with his accomplishments at such a tender age in life? Didn't his father sacrifice so much to put him through college so John could have all of the advantages that his father never had? Didn't John know how to show his gratitude? He was so ungrateful. He was too absorbed in himself and in Joan to spend time with his aging father and mother. They had sacrificed so much for John and now they had constant worries about having enough money to meet their daily expenses. They had worked themselves to exhaustion and the stress had taken its toll on their health. They had put so much money into John's college education that now there may not be enough set aside for a comfortable retirement. They constantly reminded John of their sacrifices. Occasionally, he would feel a twinge of guilt and uneasiness. Still, he would brush it off and just keep busy. After all, he had so many good things going on in his life, why worry about anything.

How did John's life deteriorate so suddenly into a panic attack? Everything in his life seemed to be totally under his control. He was unaware that there is a part of everyone's personality that we've called the *Judge*. This is the part made up of a combination of critical thoughts, memories, perceptions and physiological reactions to stress. These thoughts, memories, perceptions and stress reactions have been accumulating all of his life. He hadn't yet thought back to the time when he was eight years old in third grade and brought home his report card with a C in penmanship. He had forgotten how tense he felt standing in front of his father who was critically scrutinizing the report card. His father's eyes narrowed and his brow furrowed as he scanned the report card. John felt ever more uncomfortable the longer his father scrutinized the report card's contents. It seemed like a lifetime to John before his father finally raised his eyes from the report card. His father's eyes were narrowed into thin slits. His eyebrows turned downward in anger and disapproval, his blue eyes icy cold and glaring at John. They felt like two sharp lasers penetrating John's heart. There was nowhere to turn. He felt trapped and began to feel panic. John's hands felt cold and sweaty, his heart was racing and pounding in his chest and his muscles were so tense they started to twitch and ache.

John had felt so good about this report card. He knew he had earned an "A" in reading and in math. He was well coordinated and a good athlete so an "A" in physical education was easy to get. He had also gotten a B in spelling. His teacher liked him and often praised his work. She had smiled at him when she handed him his report card. She had told him to "keep up the good work." John had felt both excited and anxious showing his parents how well he had done. Now, his father's silent disapproval shattered all of his good feelings about his accomplishments. John felt like a "condemned" little boy. What had he done wrong that he was so unaware of? He couldn't understand what was so bad that he had to suffer in the spotlight of his father's icy cold glare. John felt frozen in panic and was totally unaware of everything else around him.

John may not remember the exact number of days his father "grounded" him, nor the number of times his father made him write, "I must do better in penmanship." Still, he will never forget the disapproving look on his father's face. This became a part of John's developing *Judge*. With his father's sarcastic words ("Can't you do better than this?"), the awful angry look on his father's face became imprinted in John's brain. This angry look combined with John's own tense panic reaction to become another experience added to the formation of the *Judge*. As these types of experiences with criticism and punishment accumulated and piled up within John, they became buried deep within his psyche. Later, this *Judge* component in his psyche would become triggered by stress, but operate psychologically outside his awareness. It could make him feel vulnerable and in a panic. It could also make him feel guilt and shame. It could make him feel trapped, hopeless and depressed because he wasn't "good enough." No matter how hard he tried or how well he did, he would never be "good enough." In John's case, no matter how well he did in everything else, his father or someone else (his doctor) would find something that was terribly wrong with him. How could John not know that, no matter how well everything was going in his life, there was something really wrong with him! This was his fate! It was dictated and controlled by his *Judge* outside his awareness.

The *Judge* in Health Maintenance

Jane was 36 years old and quite successful in her career as a businessperson. She was determined to take care of her health while enjoying the fruits of her many years of hard work in college and the launch of her successful business in public relations. She read everything she could get her hands on that discussed the latest information about diet, exercise, calcium supplementation to prevent osteoporosis, low fat foods and cholesterol free foods. She wanted the latest information about health care from all of the "experts." As it turned out, she made her approach to health maintenance an obsession. In doing so, she unwittingly turned her own health and well-being over to the *Judge*.

There is such a vast amount of health related information available to people today that it boggles the mind to try to make sense of it all. All kinds of diet information are available, from serious scientific studies to the brief ads for low-fat and low cholesterol foods. Artificial sweeteners (especially Nutrasweet®) in diet foods and beverages reinforce people's concerns about weight and getting too fat. As we know, in our society, there is a strong *Judge* on weight and being fat. This *Judge* on weight and appearance fuels obsessions with weight, diet and exercise. This *Judge* plays a major role in eating disorders of all different types — anorexia, bulimia and overeating.

With all of the attention focused on health and health maintenance, a subtle source of stress remains unnoticed. This is the *Judge* on health. It contains and conveys all of the "should" and "should not" messages regarding diet, exercise, weight, smoking, drinking, drug use and other factors thought to be related to health and health maintenance.

"The *Judge* on health care and daily health practices may be as hazardous to a person's health as an extra pat of butter or a scoop of ice cream."

The *Judge* on health care and daily health practices may be as hazardous to a person's health as an extra pat of butter or a scoop of ice cream. The *stress* induced by the guilty feelings triggered by an attack of the *health Judge* can override all of one's efforts to protect one's health. If you *feel driven* to exercise, diet compulsively and generally obsess about your health, this is especially true.

"The attitude with which you approach life overall and your health in particular can be a critical factor in affecting your health."

The attitude with which you approach life overall and your health in particular can be a critical factor in affecting your health. If your *Judge* dominates how you live and think about your health, the chronic stress which such a strong and active Judge on health maintains, it can actually become a serious problem in staying well.

So many people become preoccupied with doing their diet, exercise and health care the "right" way that they don't realize how much chronic stress they experience every day from such an active *health Judge* running their life. Just because this occurs outside their awareness doesn't mean that they are not experiencing intense stress from conflicts with the *Judge* on health and appearance.

The *Judge* and Stress

As we've seen in people's reactions triggered by the *Judge*, there is great tension, anxiety, anger, depression and other physiological reactions such as cold hands, a racing pounding heart and pain — headache or stomach ache.

Why are there such strong emotional and physical reactions to the *Judge*? It is important to keep in mind that the *Judge* originates in our childhood years under conditions of intense stress — usually criticism or punishment by a parent, teacher or caretaker. In other cases involving extreme stress — physical, emotional or sexual abuse — the stress reaction of the child is extremely severe. With repeated yelling, screaming, hitting and other scary punishing behavior by the adults in a child's life, the child's body gets conditioned to react with the stress response (fight or flight) whenever we are criticized, judged or punished. It is an automatic reflex that we have. Later, when we are teenagers or adults, we are already conditioned and programmed psychologically to react in this way to new criticism, punishment or judgment.

> **"...repeated experiences with criticism, judgment and punishment keep reinforcing our stress reaction to the *Judge*."**

Throughout our childhood and adolescence, repeated experiences with criticism, judgment and punishment keep reinforcing our stress reaction to the *Judge*. These repeated experiences make it easy for the *Judge* to take charge of us and make us feel miserable and out of control. It is as if our own stress reaction pushes the button and, presto! the *Judge* appears on the scene and takes over. It happens as quickly and simply as that!

When all of this is happening outside our awareness, we are vulnerable because we don't really know what's going on deep within our psyche. What's more, we can make ourselves feel worse if we try to be logical about it. For instance, we may tell ourselves that we are intelligent and can figure this out logically. So when we are so logical and we still can't get a handle on this intense emotional reaction to the *Judge*, this provides it with even more evidence with which to shake our confidence in managing our lives. The *Judge* then says:

> "What's the matter with you? Can't you figure this out? You're not as smart as you thought you were! In fact, you're really dumb! Any idiot with half a brain could figure this one out! I can't believe you're that stupid! Don't let anyone else know that you can't control your emotions with logic! You must really be a nut case! Don't you have any willpower over your emotions? You must really be weak!"

As the *Judge* says all of this and more, it increases our shame and misery with each critical statement.

The *Judge* in Medical Practice

Dr. Jones sat behind his sprawling desk looking over the detailed laboratory report on Mrs. Smith, a plump 45-year-old woman. She was leaning forward on the seat of her chair, obviously quite tense in anticipation of what Dr. Jones was finding in the report. Her hands were fidgeting with her purse. They were moist and sweaty. She could feel her heart racing and pounding. She never liked dealing with Dr. Jones. He always made her wait a long time before he saw her. He was cold and aloof. Sometimes Mrs. Smith would feel a chill running up and down her spine when Dr. Jones would look at her. His eyes were icy blue and she could feel no warmth or compassion from him. Dr. Jones' look reminded her so much of her father's manner. Her father had been a highly successful business executive who had little time for her. When he was around, he was also cold and aloof with no warmth or compassion. Nevertheless, Dr. Jones was considered an excellent physician and an expert in his field. So she went to him for her medical care although she felt very uncomfortable in his presence. As he looked over her laboratory report, his brow furrowed and his eyes narrowed. To Mrs. Smith, his face seemed to get bigger and bigger, the longer she sat and waited for him to speak. She could feel her anxiety increase more and more. She could hardly stand the tension as it kept building. She felt trapped and frozen in panic. He seemed totally oblivious to her obvious tension and discomfort. His aloof, cold, uncaring manner made her feel like a sick helpless child. Finally, when he did speak, he said there were some things in her report that concerned him deeply, but that they would need more tests to be absolutely certain of his diagnosis of her condition. She was shocked and terrified. What was it really and how bad was it? The thought of having to go through more tests and again having to sit in front of this cold-hearted man was more than she could bear. She typically experienced "white coat anxiety." Whenever she had her blood pressure taken at Dr. Jones' office, it measured much higher than it did when someone took it at home.

What had happened to Mrs. Smith is that she had encountered a health *Judge* in the person of her medical doctor. His *Judge* came out in his style of relating to Mrs. Smith and his other patients. He was cold, aloof, insensitive and uncaring. This personality component had very little to do with his clinical knowledge and competency as a medical doctor.

Nevertheless, Dr. Jones' *Judge* had a profound emotional effect on Mrs. Smith, inducing an intense stress reaction. The high stress level that was stirred in her provided the fuel to inflate her own *Judge*. She then felt extremely vulnerable and became convinced that something terrible was wrong with her medically. She was convinced that Dr. Jones would surely give her a fatal diagnosis. She felt totally beside herself with fear and was losing all control of herself. She wanted to jump out of her chair and run out of his office before he could pronounce his lethal diagnosis, condemning her to a slow painful death. Her *Judge* had taken her over and fueled her most terrifying fears about herself and her health.

The *Judge* and "Quackery" in Health Care

In our current health care crisis, there is so much at stake economically and in terms of people's health care and health maintenance that the debate often involves exaggerated and distorted claims from political, economic, business, clinical and even scientific perspectives. Exaggerations and distortions from politicians and health insurance/managed care business spokespersons do not surprise most lay people. What may surprise them is the extent to which health care professionals (medical doctors, psychologists and psychiatrists to name a few) will exaggerate and distort health care realities for self-serving purposes. Some scientists may engage in the same practices for political and/or financial purposes.

Of particular importance in this context are those health care professionals who set themselves up as self-appointed "experts" on medical or mental health issues. The mission of these self-appointed experts is to "protect" the health of the public from the ministrations of those practitioners whom they judge to be "quacks." The manner in which these experts operate has the classic characteristics of an extremely codependent *Judge*-dominated person. They claim to "know" what is best for everybody else. They set themselves up as the supreme authorities on health conditions and health care. They act as if they really know all there is to know about medicine, psychology and health maintenance. After all, from their perspective, nobody else could possibly have any valuable and effective health related knowledge and experience that are outside the rigid dogmatic realm that they represent.

"People with a *Judge*-dominated personality cannot tolerate uncertainty — not knowing things "for sure." They tend to fall back on cliches, making certain types of health issues much more certain than they actually are in the real world."

The grandiosity and arrogance of these self-appointed "quack-busters" suggest that some important psychological characteristics are operating, primarily a *Judge*-dominated personality. This type of personality is very rigid and operates with simplistic polarized notions of right/wrong, good/bad, true/false, healthy/sick, legitimate/quack, acceptable/not acceptable. They may even have impressive professional credentials — the right degree from a prestigious university, an impressive faculty appointment, a prestigious government or business position. Sometimes, they appear on *Nightline* or some other TV news show. They talk with great authority and they typically are hostile to alternative health care approaches that do not reflect the dogmatic views of mainstream medicine or psychiatry.

People with a *Judge*-dominated personality cannot tolerate uncertainty — not knowing things "for sure." They tend to fall back on cliches, making certain types of health issues much more certain than they actually are in the real world. These individuals possess a rigid orthodoxy and dogmatism in their thinking and are outraged by anything or anyone that questions their authority and expertise. They act as if there is absolutely no doubt in what they believe, say and do. In fact, they tend to deal in absolutes. When you listen to them, it is sometimes difficult to tell whether they are talking about health or religion.

"In fact, they tend to deal in absolutes. When you listen to them, it is sometimes difficult to tell whether they are talking about health or religion."

Although they may be talking about health and scientific issues, their bias and dogmatism belie an understanding and appreciation of the scientific and clinical enterprise. Their view of traditional medical and psychiatric practice is that they are practiced with 100 percent certainty and are entirely scientifically founded. In their view, anything outside the domain of traditional medical and psychiatric practice is, by definition, quackery. By judging and labeling any non-traditional or different health care practice as "quackery," these "experts" elevate themselves and the viewpoint they represent to the level of unquestioned authority. They reflect such contempt and disdain for any other point of view that no reasonable discussion is warranted. This is a commonly used ploy and manipulation by a controlling *Judge*-dominated personality. It is found in alcoholics, dysfunctional families and in dysfunctional organizations.

The main purpose of this ploy is either to distract or to intimidate other people in a power play.

It is useful to view the activity of the "quack-buster" in terms of the Freudian concept of "projection." By spraying the term "quack" in such a global shotgun manner on non-traditional or alternative health care practitioners, the judgmental "quack-busters" may be revealing much more about their own clinical knowledge and competence than that of others. The term "quack" may really be more reflective of the knowledge and competence of the one who judges and labels others in such a cavalier manner than that of those so harshly judged.

The nature of the psychological and physical phenomena reflected in health and disease (the mind/body connection) is so complex that it is unrealistic to believe that the narrow, rigid, simplistic views of "quack-busters" could really adequately account for these complex health-related phenomena. The knowledge and techniques developed in both the mental and physical domains of health care may be good approximations of clinical reality, but they are still inherently limited and imperfect. They don't work flawlessly for everyone. Sometimes, doctors can achieve impressive and even miraculous results through techniques in emergency medicine and in certain kinds of organ transplants. Still, we need to also recognize our limits and imperfections. However, the "quack-busters" talk as if they have access to a body of perfect knowledge and techniques. This perfectionist stance regarding a domain as complex as health functions and dysfunctions should be a signal to the listener that a *Judge* is operating under the guise of scientific and clinical expertise. The agenda of these highly codependent "quack-busters" is total control of health care practice with little or no choices open to the consumer.

As in other situations, the health-care *Judge* operates in a way that dominates others and exercises power and control. The term "quack" is used by healthcare *Judges* to put down alternative — and competing — views and techniques as tainted with heresy. They also insinuate that the motivations behind alternative health care theories and techniques are unsavory, that greed is the motivation. This ploy is used to plant seeds of doubt about the possible validity and legitimacy of alternative approaches. By using these ploys, the health care *Judges* seek to discredit alternative approaches and to block other health enhancing developments. From a financial and economic perspective, they also seek to maintain monopolistic control of the health care marketplace in which there are vast sums of money at stake. Under these conditions, the health care *Judges* operate as "quack-busters."

"From a financial and economic perspective, they also seek to maintain monopolistic control of the health care marketplace in which there are vast sums of money at stake."

Regarding these issues, recent developments in science and mathematics help us to understand some inherent limitations and imperfections when we are dealing with complex natural and health care phenomena. These new developments have been beautifully described by author James Gleick in his book *Chaos: Making a New Science.*

The *Judge* in Catastrophic Illness

An individual we met at a conference, but did not have as a client in therapy, was involved in leading a cancer support group. Yet, when her own cancer reoccurred, she viewed it as punishment for "not being good enough." She had done all the "right things" to be a good example to her group. She wanted to show the group members that, if you eat right, exercise, meditate and do other "healthy" things, then you deserve to heal and recover. She felt devastated and ashamed when her cancer recurred. "Doing all the right healthy things" just wasn't good enough to prevent a recurrence of her cancer.

Further discussion with her revealed that she felt "not good enough" all of her life. This was just another example that she didn't do things quite well enough. Outside her awareness, she was trying so hard to do things exactly the way the experts said to keep the cancer at bay and under her control. Unwittingly, she was providing evidence to her *Judge* that, no matter how hard she tried to do all of the "right" things to maintain good health, she still didn't do them well enough; therefore, she deserved to be sick again. She still was not perfect enough and certainly "not good enough." Therefore, her *Judge* condemned her to a recurrence of the cancer. Unless this woman deals with her strong *Judge* and its destructive messages, all of the modern technology of medicine may not be enough to stop her progression of cancer.

The *Judge* in the Training
of Health Care Professionals

Medical doctors frequently have a similar dilemma involving the *Judge* because it so often operates outside their awareness. The training of doctors frequently occurs under highly stressful conditions involving life and death decisions. Many young medical students learn that a good doctor is God-like with omnipotent power over life and death. This God-like doctor must know all of the right answers, must never make a mistake, must be perfect, must not need much sleep and have no human weaknesses.

Such a training system unwittingly contributes to the formation of grandiose thinking with feelings of omnipotence and omniscience. Unfortunately, these are also some of the characteristics of the *Judge*. A paradox is created in which scientific and clinical knowledge blended with high technology may also be combined with grandiose and rigid thinking. This is so typical of the 8 year-old emotional and intellectual developmental level of the *Judge*. These create conditions which are very conducive to establishing and maintaining the active presence of the *Judge* in health care institutions. Holding the belief that they must be God-like can be highly destructive emotionally to medical students. If a patient dies, they may view it as a personal failure. They may have an exaggerated need to control the outcome of illness and to keep people from dying at all costs, regardless of the quality of the patient's life.

When medical conditions are simple and clear, this type of dysfunctional system may still work satisfactorily to the benefit of most individual patients. But, as more and more uncertainty enters the case, the impact of the doctor's *Judge* will likely become greater and greater. Defensiveness may increase as questions mount and no clear answers are apparent. Other alternative approaches will often be dismissed in an arrogant judgmental manner. Disparaging judgmental remarks may be made about these alternative health care approaches and practices, adding to the patient's anxiety.

As medical students progress through such a demanding and often dysfunctional system, many of them experience impairment of their own health from constant stress and neglecting their own basic human needs. For example, they frequently don't eat or sleep properly. Ironically, in all of their years of medical training, since they have been taught so little about good clinical nutrition, especially for people working under highly stressful conditions, they lack some of the most basic knowledge needed to take care of themselves.

Medical students and interns often work extremely long hours, frequently being deprived of sleep. They may be subject to humiliating criticism when they make mistakes. They must either be perfect or else they are worthless, a good-bad dichotomy which is characteristic of the criticisms of the *Judge*. The words of author Joan Borysenko, Ph.D. are apropos here in describing her own professional school experience at the Harvard Medical School. "I was a relentless perfectionist, trying to control and succeed at everything. I was a physical wreck...I was a hard-headed scientist literally killing myself to master the ways of the medical establishment." (pp. 1-2)

One medical student we know recently had two auto accidents and totaled her car because she fell asleep at the wheel after extremely long on-call assignments at the hospital. Fortunately, she wasn't killed or severely injured. Others students or interns may turn to drugs to help them stay awake or they will fall asleep on the job. Many students develop stress-related diseases. And, always, there is the ever present *Judge* operating within and around them in their colleagues, their supervisors, and in the very institution in which they train. These are conditions which make many doctors in training at risk for addiction to prescription or other drugs in order to cope with the stress of their arduous training.

"These are conditions which make many doctors in training at risk for addiction to prescription or other drugs in order to cope with the stress of their arduous training."

Young doctors often see drugs as a good answer to their stress, pain and anxiety. Thus, recommending addicting drugs to their patients is much easier for them. This helps to perpetuate what author Anne Wilson Schaef calls an addictive dysfunctional system.

Doctors who are less *Judge*-dominated and see themselves as facilitators of the healing process tend to be less "ego-involved." That is, they have less of a personalized investment in the outcome and can be more appropriately detached, but still convey warmth and caring for the person under their care. Such an approach is compatible with Yoga philosophy — give your very best service with love and let go of the outcome.

"A system that repeatedly humiliates and abuses subordinate persons is, by definition, a dysfunctional system."

There is nothing that is naturally inherent in medical doctor training which requires students to be treated with humiliation and abuse. Any system that repeatedly humiliates and abuses subordinate persons is, by definition, a dysfunctional system. Given the dysfunctional nature of some aspects of medical training, it is remarkable that so many good outcomes do occur. Still, there are far too many cases in which the *Judge*-dominated dysfunctional nature of the medical training system has many adverse effects. Patients and doctors may become addicted to prescription medications. Hazardous and sometimes lethal prescription drug interactions may occur. Arrogant judgmental debunking of alternative health care approaches may prevent a patient from obtaining effective treatment. Over-medicating a patient, especially in psychiatry and geriatrics is not uncommon.

Today, there are a growing number of courageous and determined doctors who are pioneering a different type of healing. They tend to have what we have called "S" type personalities, having encapsulated their *Judge*, or they have had "spiritual awakening" experiences. They are doing work that integrates body, mind and spirit energy, encouraging patients to heal their lives and relationships, not just their physical disease.

Often, the physical disease heals as well, but that is not always the primary aim. If it is the patient's choice to die, they help him or her to accept and be peaceful with this choice, finish and release worldly attachments and be allowed to "leave" in a dignified manner when he or she is ready. Dr. Bernie Siegel, author of *Love, Medicine and Miracles* and *Peace, Love and Healing*, is a primary example of this approach. Bernie often describes his family of origin as being very close, loving and nonjudgmental.

Other examples of doctors are Brugh Joy, author of *Joy's Way* and Leonard Laskow, author of *Healing with Love*. Dr. Andrew Weil talks about a very different type of medical training which essentially would drastically diminish the presence of the *Judge* in health care. Hopefully, these men will have an impact on the training of young doctors and begin to change the medical system in the direction of a more sensitive healing system with much less domination by the *Judge*.

"Hopefully, these men will have an impact on the training of young doctors and begin to change the medical system in the direction of a more sensitive healing system with much less domination by the *Judge*."

The *Judge* in Training Psychologists

We have also had an opportunity to observe the *Judge's* influence on the training of clinical psychologists. For nearly fifteen years, at our office, we have worked with graduate students in counseling and clinical psychology. In the training of psychologists, there is usually a very heavy emphasis on theory and research. The highly academic and intellectual nature of psychology graduate programs has a strong tendency to reinforce the *Judge* in these students, often outside the awareness of both faculty and students. This occurs because the *Judge* typically relies on verbal skills and manipulation. In a highly intellectual and verbal enterprise such as a graduate program in psychology, the *Judge* may become activated outside a person's awareness.

"The highly academic and intellectual nature of psychology graduate programs has a strong tendency to reinforce the *Judge* in these students, often outside the awareness of both faculty and students."

One student with whom we worked had great difficulty tolerating being in a therapy group as part of the training experience. The student felt that because he had passed all of his psychology courses with A's, he should know more about what was happening in the group than the lay people — the group members themselves, especially those who had a great deal of experience in group therapy and personal growth. The student's *Judge* could not accept the fact that many clients in the group could know so much more practical psychology than this straight A student. As part of his psychology academic training, the student had come to believe that psychological knowledge is esoteric and only the "privileged" few who study it academically and professionally could possibly know enough about it to understand it.

Since the essentials of psychological knowledge — human emotion and behavior — are a part of everyone's experience, it is impossible for this knowledge to be kept secret and limited to professional psychologists. Every one of us learns a great deal about psychology just in the natural processes of growing up in a family, in school, in relationships and in a job. Those who do become professional psychologists, psychiatrists, social workers, counselors and other mental health professionals can become very vulnerable to the *Judge* on psychological knowledge. By becoming a mental health professional, we provide evidence to the *Judge* that we have a certain amount of specialized academic knowledge and expertise in psychology. Some of us even have licenses to demonstrate to the world that we are really experts in psychology. Therefore, when we have personal psychological problems with low self-esteem, depression, anxiety attacks, relationships or parenting, we are fair game for our *Judge* to attack us: "After all, if you are such an expert in psychology and mental health, why do you have these personal problems? What's wrong with you?"

Beyond the *Judge:* Mentoring & Aging

When Rick was in graduate school at the University of Illinois, he had the good fortune to learn psychology under the training and mentoring of the late Dr. T. Ernest Newland. Dr. Newland was already in his sixties when Rick started his work toward a Ph.D. in School Psychology. What made this graduate education and training experience especially rewarding for Rick was that Ernie had so much knowledge and experience to offer to his students. Ernie was a brilliant diagnostician who loved the challenge of figuring out difficult problems. He was always curious and open to new ideas; he also knew a great deal about the early developments in the field of psychology and what their historical place was. This was important to him and he felt that it was valuable for his students to understand and appreciate this, too. He used to say that his younger colleagues among the faculty were "rediscovering the wheel and rushing to get their 'new' discoveries into print" in the professional journals. They lacked Ernie's historical awareness and perspective.

One of Ernie's most important characteristics was that he was confident and secure in himself professionally. He readily gave encouragement and he took great pride in the accomplishments of his students. He also accepted them as equals intellectually and professionally although very few of them matched his imposing 6 feet, 4 inches figure. Our son, Alan, used to call Ernie the "big Bear" because, to a two- or three-year-old child, Ernie looked huge. Ernie liked to play the devil's advocate and raise challenging questions, taking nothing for granted. He encouraged us to maintain our curiosity, emphasizing that there is so much to learn, no matter how old you are. Nobody can ever really know it all. Yet, most importantly, he told us to make sure that something makes sense to you. If it doesn't, keep an open mind, but also keep asking questions. In this way, Ernie was a wonderful mentor as well as an outstanding professor. He aged with great dignity and class. We think that related to his longevity. Ernie died a few years ago at the age of 89. His life spanned many decades and he realized how important it is for a person to share his or her knowledge and experience with younger people. What made his mentoring very special was that it was done with great mutual respect and it was *Judge*-free. Ernie was a wonderful example of the truly wise and mature man whose *Warrior* kept his *Judge* at bay so that he could freely share his wealth of knowledge and experience with others.

> **"What made his mentoring very special was that it was done with great mutual respect and it was *Judge*-free."**

CHAPTER 10

THE *JUDGE* IN INDIVIDUAL AND SOCIAL CHANGE

In August of 1995, Rick had an opportunity to present the basic concepts in this book at the *National Depression and Manic-Depression Association's* Annual Conference in Chicago. His presentation included the basic model described earlier relating the *Judge*, the *inner child* and the *Warrior* archetype. The model seemed to make much sense to many people in the audience. Still, one man raised a concern. He said that the model and the process of applying it seemed to be "too simple" for such psychiatric disorders as depression or anxiety and panic attacks. He believed that there had to be something more complicated and esoteric to account for so much psychological distress. How could it possibly be so simple?

Our experience and the experience of many of our clients show that this is, indeed, a simple model with concepts that are easy for most people to grasp. It is nearly twenty years since we were first introduced to the concept of the *Judge* by Dr. John Cooper. Through our own personal therapy as well as through our professional therapy work with hundreds of clients, we have come to appreciate this unique psychological concept with all of its many nuances and implications. Grasping this concept really is easy because we can all relate it to our own experience. It also makes good psychological sense to relate the concept of the *Judge* to the concept of the *inner child*. The dominant relationship of the *Judge* over the *inner child* accounts for depression, low self-esteem, lack of confidence, anxiety and panic disorder and obsessive thinking and behavior. When we relate both the *Judge* and the *inner child* to the *Warrior* archetype and to a person's spirituality, we have a very strong psychological model with which to work. We have seen dramatic shifts in people during a workshop when they have succeeded in shrinking their *Judge* and the *Warrior* archetype emerges with great strength and spirituality.

"The *Judge* is everywhere. It is all around us and it is also within us psychologically."

We have shown how the *Judge* is related to intense stress, low self-esteem, depression and panic attacks. We don't believe that it has to be made more complicated and esoteric than this because the *Judge* is so much a part of our experience as human beings. Our hope is that, because the concept of the *Judge* is basically quite simple and common to human experience, we can share it with large numbers of people. Its application will then make a substantial positive difference in many people's lives. We believe that it can be applied in a variety of settings from individual psychotherapy to intimate relationships to larger organizations — business, professional and governmental. The *Judge* is everywhere. It is all around us as well as within us psychologically.

"Psychiatric Diagnosis Comes *Alive*"

We recently received a brochure in the mail from *American Psychiatric Press, Inc.* marketing some new books, audio tapes and video tapes related to psychiatry's new diagnostic "Bible" — the DSM-IV. When we received this brochure, something struck us as rather odd, but, at first, we weren't quite sure what it was. Looking at the brochure again, it became clear to us what we found so disturbing about it. The title *Psychiatric Diagnosis Comes Alive* says a great deal about contemporary psychiatric and mental health approaches and attitudes. Apparently, for some professionals, it is more important that a psychiatric diagnosis "comes *alive*" than whether the person to whom they apply the diagnostic label "comes *alive*." In some mental health settings, because of health insurance and managed care requirements, the intellectual exercise of making a diagnosis is more important than the therapeutic process that helps people to shrink their *Judge* and come alive. Paradoxically, the intellectual exercise of applying a psychiatric diagnosis often feeds the *Judge* in the mental health practitioner and in the client. When this occurs, it does not serve the client well.

From the perspective we have described in this book, the concept of the *Judge* cuts across many of these arbitrary psychiatric diagnostic labels given in DSM-IV. It is the *Judge* that blocks feelings and aliveness in people, not a psychiatric diagnostic label. The concept of the *Judge* and the model we have described in this book makes the DSM-IV diagnostic labels irrelevant to doing the type of effective psychotherapy that will truly help a person "come *alive*" emotionally.

"...the concept of the *Judge* cuts across many of these arbitrary psychiatric diagnostic labels given in DSM-IV."

The model utilizing the *Judge* concept can be effectively used to psychologically empower people to take responsible control over their lives, giving them a clearer direction in developing much more of their full human potential. For many people, they can apply this model to help free their creativity, their spirituality and their aliveness from the emotional blocks and destructive effects of the *Judge*. Therapeutically, it can be used to heal emotional scars and wounds and to support recovery from addiction and codependence.

The Mental Health Continuum
———— ∞∞❀❀∞∞ ————

   This book has presented a new psychological model that applies to everyone's psychological development and functioning. Although the concept of the *Judge* and the model presented here were developed in a clinical psychology practice, these concepts are applicable to everyone. This includes people who have been psychologically diagnosed with emotional or behavioral problems as well as most other people who do not experience such severe problems that they seek professional help.

   The model has three components which are interrelated psychologically: the *Judge*, the *inner child* and the *Warrior* archetype. These components are found in everyone's personality. When the *Judge* is activated and dominates the *inner child*, a person experiences more stress and more psychological disturbance. This can happen to anybody. It is part of our human nature and the way we respond to different situations. For some people, these reactions can be so disturbing and debilitating that professional help may be needed to help them recover and to cope better. Other people may feel the impact of their *Judge's* wrath being stirred and threatening their *inner child*. Nevertheless, they are able to cope and continue to function without professional help. Their experience is part of everyday life. Therefore, the model may be considered either as a mental health clinical psychology model or it may be considered to be a general psychological model that is closely related to stress.

   As a general psychological model, we may view it as part of everyone's personality development and it is intimately related to human nature. We can teach and apply the model as a part of education for life experience. In other words, it is important for everyone to know something about this psychological model and how it affects each of us – our stress reactions, our relationships, our self-esteem, our self-confidence, our moods, etc.

We believe that this model would be a valuable addition to education programs at different grade and developmental levels. It could easily be incorporated into courses in social studies and psychology, health, literature, art, drama, etc.

THE MENTAL HEALTH CONTINUUM

Judge Free	Normal Personality	Health Problems	Inflated Judge

The *Judge* in Sports

We believe that one major reason why sports have so much appeal to many of us is that they help us learn to cope with ambiguity and uncertainty in life. The outcome is uncertain, but we build in ways to keep score and determine a definite winner and a loser. Still, wittingly or unwittingly, wherever we are active in keeping score or counting, the *Judge* has an opportunity to take charge. The sports world often gives us some good examples of the *Judge* at work. Yet sometimes in sports, we also see examples of reducing the domination of the *Judge* over athletic performance. In the relatively rare situations when this does occur, there are some interesting and exciting improvements in natural athletic performance and success.

During the 1995 season of the National Football League, one of the most interesting and exciting stories was the emergence of Jim Harbaugh as a star quarterback and leader of the Indianapolis Colts. Most football fans know that Harbaugh played for two of the most demanding (and possibly *Judge*-dominated) coaches — Bo Schembechler in college and

Mike Ditka with the Chicago Bears. Harbaugh was a good capable player under those coaches, but he really came into his own, playing under the Colts' coach, Ted Marchibroda. Marchibroda is probably as *Judge*-free a man as you'll find in the ranks of football coaches. His warmth and encouragement brought out the very best in Harbaugh's play as he led his team into the 1995 NFL playoffs and within a heartbeat of Superbowl XXX. When he picked Harbaugh to be his top quarterback, Marchibroda's words of encouragement to him were, "Let 'er rip!" This meant, "Just be yourself and let all of your natural talent and instincts come out to the best of your ability." Harbaugh's 1995 record under coach Marchibroda speaks for itself. In our view, however, the key to their success together was that coach Marchibroda took the *Judge* off Harbaugh's shoulders so that he could really play to the level of his natural potential.

"...one of his greatest successes was to reduce the impact of the *Judge* on himself and his players."

Here is another example of this process. In 1995, Phil Jackson, the coach of the Chicago Bulls NBA basketball team, wrote *Sacred Hoops*. In his book he describes his own development and how he applied what he learned to coaching this outstanding basketball team. Jackson's story is an excellent example of how he used spiritual principles to work with his players, raising their level of individual performance for the benefit of the entire team. In our view, one of his greatest successes was to reduce the impact of the *Judge* on himself and his players. By removing the dominance of the *Judge* over individual and team performance, the Chicago Bulls have enjoyed outstanding success in the 1990's. From our viewpoint, a fascinating sidelight to the Bulls' success is that their logo, a snarling frowning Bull image, is also a *Judge* image. Every time they stepped on their home floor to play a game in the old Chicago Stadium or at the new United Center in Chicago, the image of the Bull *Judge* was on the basketball court. During the many games we watched the Bulls play, we often wondered whether the image of the Bull *Judge* on the court had anything to do with the Bulls' opponents missing key shots at crucial points in the game.

The *Judge*, The *Warrior*, and the Green Jacket: Lessons from the Masters Tournament

When Tiger Woods won the 1997 Masters Golf Tournament at the age of 21, his amazing accomplishment was heralded around the world. What Tiger accomplished in the 1997 Masters was an impressive athletic feat for anyone, let alone a 21-year-old playing in his first Masters as a professional golfer. Throughout the four days of the tournament, the manner in which he played and kept his composure when paired with older more experienced players was especially impressive. Logic and experience told us that the pressure of playing for the championship of this most prestigious of golf tournaments should have adversely affected Tiger's play. After all, in the 1996 Masters, we saw what the pressure in the final round did to as great and seasoned a veteran player as Greg Norman. Yet, amazingly, in round after round, Tiger played brilliantly. Not only did he not crumble under the pressure, but he seemed to thrive on it, becoming stronger as he played. Ironically, the older more experienced players seemed to wither under the pressure. There must be some lessons here for all of us who watched and were thrilled by Tiger's magnificent performance.

The last two Masters tournaments are, indeed, instructive to us. We learn both through the excellence of the golf we watched and also in the psychology of the game and life itself. The contrast between Tiger's final round of the 1997 Masters and that of Greg Norman in the 1996

Masters is truly remarkable. How was it possible for a beginning professional golfer like Tiger Woods to maintain such incredible poise and composure competing with the top professional golfers in the world while in the spotlight of the TV cameras broadcasting his performance to every corner of the world? Who among us who are golf fans can ever forget what happened to Greg Norman on that final Sunday of the 1996 Masters? After the first three rounds of the tournament, Norman was leading by six strokes going into that final round. He had played confidently and brilliantly, shooting an opening round of 63 to jump into the lead which he held until the final day. We could all identify with the feelings that Norman must have felt as he was getting so close to finally winning the coveted green jacket, emblematic of the Masters championship. Then we watched in disbelief as his dream was shattered in a matter of minutes. Soon, it even became emotionally painful to continue to watch this great player's game disintegrate right before our eyes. It was like watching a close relative or friend slowly dying a hopeless and painful death. Norman had gone from shooting a phenomenal 63 Thursday to shooting a 78 in the final round Sunday, finishing five strokes behind Nick Faldo's winning score. What had happened to Norman struck a universal cord in all of us. We all have intuitively known the feelings and the type of situation he experienced that day. Very few players will ever have the thrill of playing in the Masters, let alone leading by six strokes going into the final round. Nevertheless, we can all relate to being so close to getting something we desperately want and then having it denied to us. In fact, Norman's painful disappointment at again being denied a green jacket brought out a rallying response from many of his fellow professional golfers and from the public. In our own unique way, we could all relate to what he had experienced.

What could account for such dramatic differences in play and in the outcome for two such gifted golfers? We can discount both age and professional experience as explanations for what we had witnessed in the final round of the Masters in two consecutive years. Both Tiger Woods and Greg Norman had clearly demonstrated that they each had the necessary <u>physical</u> skills to play superb rounds of golf on Augusta National. So it must have been something in the mental or psychological part of the game that spelled the difference in their play on the final Sunday of the tournament.

There is a simple, but profound psychological explanation for what we witnessed in these last two Masters tournaments. This psychological explanation draws from our model using the concepts of the *Judge*, the *Warrior* and the *inner child*. This model shows us how the *Judge* can dominate, control, threaten and intimidate our *inner child*. When this happens deep within our psyche, we become more and more tense, increasing our stress level dramatically. As our tension and stress increase, we lose our self-confidence and our natural rhythm in whatever we are doing. We become distracted. We lose our focus. We start to think too much about our most natural movements and instincts. We lose touch with our "flow."

"...the *Judge* is that internal driving psychological force that can dominate our lives, preventing us from experiencing more joy and satisfaction in life."

How does this psychological thing we call the *Judge* affect sports and athletic performance? For all of us, the *Judge* is that internal driving psychological force that can dominate our lives, preventing us from experiencing more joy and satisfaction in life. When the *Judge* is in control over our *inner child*, no amount of money, no amount of education, no amount of physical skill and talent, not even our accomplishments are ever enough to meet the *Judge*'s insatiable demands for perfection.

For those of us who are not professional golfers, we all know what it is like to stand on the first tee ready to hit our first shot when there are people watching us. It sometimes seems like there are a thousand eyes all watching as we stand over our ball getting ready to take our first swing. The more we are conscious and aware of all of those eyes watching as we start our back swing, the more tense we become. We may notice that we are too much into our head thinking about our swing, rather than trusting our natural flow and instincts to carry it out. We just hope and pray that we make good contact with the ball and get off the first tee without flubbing the ball and making a total fool of ourselves. This is what it's like when the *Judge* is stirred up in our psyche as we're about to hit the golf ball. We become so distracted that everything that we have done so naturally before has become a struggle and takes extra effort.

"We become so distracted that everything that we have done so naturally before has become a struggle and takes extra effort."

In contrast to our feeling the *Judge* scrutinizing our *inner child*, when the mature *Warrior* part of our personality comes to the fore, we feel exhilarated, supremely confident, fearless, relaxed, focused and in a natural "flow." This is when we are at our very best. This is when we can play to our fullest potential. We don't even have to think about what we are doing. It just comes naturally with a minimum of effort. We can now enjoy the adrenaline rush without becoming overcome by it. When the *Judge* takes us over, bringing on more stress, that kind of adrenaline rush becomes uncontrollable. The combination of so much tension and stress with too much adrenaline flowing breaks down our natural skills and ability to perform and execute the most basic shots. We are no longer our natural selves. We may lose control of our game. It gets away from us and getting it back is difficult. As the *Judge* takes us over outside our awareness, our increasing stress and tension provide the *Judge* with more energy to keep itself inflated like a huge balloon with a scary face distracting and terrorizing our *inner child*.

> **"...when the mature *Warrior* part of our personality comes to the fore, we feel exhilarated, supremely confident, fearless, relaxed, focused and in a natural 'flow'."**

Earlier in the book in Chapter 2, we described Fred's experience of a *Judge* attack. As Fred became desensitized to the automatic reflex response to a *Judge* attack, he started to recognize the situations in which his *Judge's* wrath was stirred up. "When I get close to getting what I really want," he observed, "something that is so good, then the fear of 'losing it' intensifies." This is a good example of the *Judge* taking over and blocking us from experiencing a great accomplishment and more satisfying things in life. It is also a good explanation of what happened at the the Masters tournament and the final round performances of Tiger Woods and Greg Norman. Watching the final round of the 1996 Masters tournament, all the viewers were aware of how desperately Greg Norman wanted to win his first green jacket. This is an example of how the *Judge* goes to work on us, taking us over psychologically, creating more and more stress and tension. This is how the *Judge* blocks us from experiencing greater success and accomplishment of a truly special goal.

When we become aware of our *Judge*, we can learn to confront it and shrink it so that it loses its power and control over our lives and our athletic performance. When we can draw on our mature *Warrior* part of our personality, we can shrink our *Judge* and its domination over our *inner child*. This frees us emotionally to use more of our natural talents and abilities without the tension and distractions brought on by the *Judge*. This allows us to perform to the very best of our natural abilities and skills. This is what Tiger Woods accomplished at the tender age of 21. He brought up the mature *Warrior* part of his personality to keep his *Judge* from taking him over. His *Warrior* kept him focused and in the flow of his game. It was very subtle, but very powerful. In fact, Tiger Woods' *Warrior* energy and focus overwhelmed his nearest competitors and they fell victim to their own *Judge*. Their games fell apart as their *Judge* took more and more control.

Tiger Woods also had the benefit of the advice and support of "Fluff," his caddy, who could draw on knowledge and experience at Augusta National and other big golf tournaments. Fluff was like a mentor to Tiger, advising him at crucial times and helping to keep Tiger's emotions under control so that his *Judge* did not take over and destroy his game. Instead, Tiger's *Warrior* was in charge and we were treated to the spectacle of an historic and phenomenal round of golf, culminated by the final putt on the 18th green to set the tournament record at 18 under par.

What we can learn from the last two Masters tournaments is that the *Judge* can take over anyone at anytime, especially when we are so close to getting what we most desperately want. In fact, the closer we are to getting it is when the *Judge* is most likely to assert itself and take control of us if it can. And the more the *Judge* takes control of us, the more difficult it is to release its destructive grip on our *inner child*. It can block us and shatter our most precious of dreams and accomplishments. The *Judge* can be so unfeeling and cruel, inflicting the most painful of disappointments on us. Age has nothing to do with whether the *Judge* takes us over. It is our own awareness and coping mechanisms which make the ultimate difference in what happens. In fact, the *Judge* can also exploit the age and experience factor. It can convince the older more experienced player that he should be able to handle the pressure and intimidate the younger, less experienced player. If the older more experienced player buys into this *Judge* message, he is in trouble. We saw this happen in round after round with Tiger's playing partners who fell further and further behind. Colin Montgomerie, Tiger's playing partner Saturday, probably believed this *Judge* message more than any other player. Starting the Saturday round only three strokes behind Tiger, Colin finished 24 strokes behind Tiger at the end of the tournament Sunday! Colin lost 21 strokes to Tiger in two days!

Just as age has nothing to do with whether the *Judge* takes us over, age is not always a factor in whether the *Warrior* emerges and carries us along fearlessly and with a clear focus on what we are doing. Tiger Woods proved that he could draw on *Warrior* energy and use it consistently to carry him to a phenomenal victory in one of the most prestigious golf tournaments, earning a green jacket, emblematic of the Masters champion. Only a handful of men will ever have the experience of playing in the Masters and even fewer of winning a green jacket at Augusta National, but every one of us can learn to shrink our *Judge*'s control and domination over our lives. Each of us can learn to bring out our own mature *Warrior* to empower us psychologically from within so that we can each become all that we can be.

The *Judge* and Spirituality

The *Judge* is an especially useful concept that can enable us to distinguish between deep, warm spirituality and cold *Judge*-dominated morality in various religions and cultures. The experience of true spirituality is felt as warm, nurturing, life-affirming and life-supporting. It also has a solid feel to it in contrast to an inner emptiness. A spiritually strong philosophy or religion is life enhancing, whereas cold, *Judge*-dominated morality is experienced as devoid of emotion and feels ominous and threatening. There is often an emotional deadness and numbness despite an elaborate rational theology and centuries of tradition.

The origin of religion has been compared to hot lava flowing from the inner sources, often an enlightenment experience of the religion's founder. As the centuries pass, however, this enlightenment experience becomes transformed into dogma (the lava cools and hardens) and the original inspiration is lost. It becomes an outward rigid form with no inner aliveness. The core becomes empty and dead. This has happened to all religious traditions around the world; they become more judgmental and less spiritual over time. Then, a new leader becomes inspired and starts a new branch of the religion. The new followers feel closer to Spirit and the process repeats itself over time. Awareness of this pattern could prevent religious groups from killing each other over the idea of "my religion is better than your religion!" Shrinking the *Judge* in religions could potentially prevent religious abuse and, perhaps, even Holy War.

The *Judge* in Social and Cultural Development

When Rick was in graduate school, one book he found most fascinating was *Magic, Science and Religion* by Bronislaw Malinowski. In retrospect, this book has even more relevance for us now in understanding the *Judge* in social and cultural development. In technologically less well developed societies, simplistic, magical types of thinking are often used to explain events. Yet since the *Age of Reason*, when modern science began to emerge and develop its own philosophy and methods, we assumed that reason and the scientific method would solve most of the basic problems of life. The "good" society would not be too far behind reason and scientific discoveries.

Without an awareness of the psychological phenomenon of the *Judge*, it was easy to assume that, if people could develop *reason* and learn the scientific method by means of education, intellectual and academic development and scientific activity, they could transcend the limitations of "primitive" irrational thinking described by Malinowski and other anthropologists. It was easy to see the limitations of concrete either-or types of thinking that were sometimes observed in these supposedly more primitive cultures. Yet it is much more difficult to see that certain simplistic types of logical, verbal reasoning are also ploys of the *Judge*. This is especially true when the *Judge*, operating in the personality of well-educated business people or professional adults in our society, succeeds in gathering enough evidence or data to make a convincing point in a power play with their business or professional colleagues.

In Western culture, we have a tendency to believe that logic and reason are the highest type of intellectual and psychological development. We organize our educational system to train our children so that they think and act with logic and reason. However, unwittingly, over the centuries, we have sown the seeds for fueling and reinforcing *Judge*-dominated thinking throughout the development of Western culture and education. In the process, we have suppressed intuition and emotion as a way of "knowing."

"In Western culture, we have a tendency to believe that logic and reason are the highest type of intellectual and psychological development."

From this perspective, it makes more sense to say that a person, society or culture has reached a higher level of development when they have become *Judge*-free in contrast to *Judge*-dominated. By psychological definition, the *Judge* is always operating from a child "ego state." When individuals, societies or cultures shrink the influence of the *Judge* over their lives, they are operating at a much freer emotional level and at a higher spiritual level than is possible when the *Judge* dominates. They are also operating at a much more mature intellectual level developmentally. This allows them to move beyond the "either-or" simplistic form of thinking and to explore the subtleties and uncertainties of life.

"As we develop psychologically in childhood, we go through stages that set the foundation for the *Judge* to emerge in our adult personality."

Realistically, becoming *Judge*-free is an ideal because of two factors. One factor concerns the manner in which we are "wired" neurologically and psychologically. As we develop psychologically in childhood, we go through stages that set the foundation for the *Judge* to emerge in our adult personality. Between eight and ten years of age, we go through a very concrete stage of "either/or" thinking. This type of "either/or" concrete thinking is exactly the thinking style of the *Judge*. Later in life, when we become stressed and come under the influence of the *Judge* in our personality, we have a tendency to revert to this early developmental stage. The *Judge* does not allow for the gray areas of ambiguity and uncertainty in life. Nor does the *Judge* allow for any mitigating circumstances. It has no feeling nor compassion.

The other major factor is that our culture and society are so *Judge*-dominated that finding people and places which are not profoundly affected by the *Judge* is very difficult. When the author, Ann Wilson Schaef, describes the *Addicted Society*, she is really describing a *Judge*-dominated society. The *Addicted Society* is synonymous with the *Judge*-dominated society because the *Judge* is the underlying psychological fuel or trigger which drives addictive and codependent behaviors.

Western societies and cultures have raised intellectual, scientific, cultural and academic development to such a high level of value while grossly neglecting the importance of emotional and spiritual development. The combination of overemphasis on the intellectual, scientific and academic while neglecting the importance of the emotional and the spiritual contributes substantially to dominance of the *Judge* in all areas of a culture and society, including individual psychological functioning.

> **"Western societies and cultures have raised intellectual, scientific, cultural and academic development to a high level of value while grossly neglecting the importance of emotional and spiritual development."**

In this century, most of us have been utterly shocked and horrified by the indescribable barbarity of the Holocaust and other atrocities committed by the Nazis. We have also been baffled. Inevitably we have to ask ourselves, "How could such an 'advanced,' highly developed and 'rational' society like Germany's have perpetrated such heinous crimes and horrors?" It is true that Germany was quite advanced intellectually, scientifically, culturally and academically. Still, German society and culture are historically so strongly *Judge*-dominated that, under certain conditions such as existed under Hitler and the Nazis, the *Judge* came to totally dominate all of Europe. The *Judge*-dominated Nazis, especially the *SS*, literally condemned millions of Jews and other people to death. They carried out their diabolical plans in a cold-blooded, calculated, methodical way as only the *Judge* could.

When a society or culture overemphasizes the intellectual, scientific and academic while neglecting the importance of the emotional well-

being and the spirituality of its people, there is much greater risk for
the *Judge* to become dominant in all areas of that culture and society,
including individual psychological functioning and family systems.
This is analogous to the body builder who becomes "muscle bound"
for lack of balance in overall development and physical activities.
In our culture, we are "*Judge*-bound" or *Judge*-dominated. This means
that the *Judge* has become so dominant in individual personality
functioning, family dynamics, institutions and organizations that it
shapes virtually every aspect of our lives. We maintain intense sources
of stress on children, adolescents and adults in nearly all of our cultural
institutions. We have very strong beliefs that there is a right way to
raise children and a right way to teach and to train children. The more
rigid and insensitive we are in applying these beliefs to child rearing
and to teaching, the more pressure our children feel from the *Judge*
in us.

"A major way in which we institutionalize the *Judge* is by becoming dependent on so-called experts who supposedly have all the right answers for us."

A major way in which we institutionalize the *Judge* is by becoming
dependent on so-called experts who supposedly have all the right
answers for us. Of course, we have well educated, experienced and
wise individuals who can teach and guide us. We have a strong tendency
to put many of these people on pedestals and to become completely
dependent on their opinions as if they were divine truth handed down
on Mt. Sinai. This sets up a codependent relationship between us and
these experts. The expert often becomes the carrier of judgmental
opinions and beliefs that we allow to dominate our parenting and
teaching behaviors. We become preoccupied with doing our parenting

the right way as if we are being observed and evaluated by these experts. When this happens to us, it adversely affects our spontaneity and intuition in relating to our own children. We often have to stop ourselves and think about whether we are saying and doing the right things with our children "according to the experts." This process of depending on experts also undermines our own sense of personal power. We give up responsibility for ourselves and our own behavior. We allow the *Judge* to take over the direction of our parenting and child care. When this occurs, it often leads to more frequent power struggles between parents and children. This can often have dire psychological consequences.

Human beings have a tremendous capacity for adaptation and resilience in coping with stress. However, the *Judge* in our parents, teachers, clergy and other authorities attempts to break the child's spirit and undermines the natural resilience with which a child is born. The rigidity of the *Judge* is the antithesis of the spontaneity and resilience of the natural child. The *Judge's* goal is to block the natural child's development and the unfolding of its full potential in all areas of life.

"The *Judge's* goal is to block the natural child's development and the unfolding of its full potential in all areas of life."

When adults are operating from a *Judge*-dominated place, they are really coming from a frightened little child place and they have a major issue with trust. Such adults don't trust themselves and certainly don't trust anyone else. The more the *Judge* dominates our lives, the more difficulties we have with trust. We don't really trust ourselves nor do we easily trust others. We have a strong need to always be right and to know things with absolute certainty to feel safe and secure.

Ambiguity and uncertainty are very difficult to tolerate if we constantly live under the rule and the threat of the *Judge*. Yet, ambiguity and uncertainty are inherent in the life process. The *Judge* drives us to be more controlling so that we don't have to feel the anxiety that ambiguity and uncertainty may trigger. The more the *Judge* dominates us, the less we trust our own intuition and the more we try to be completely logical and rational. So often, when logic and rational approaches to solving life's problems don't work out, we become baffled and frustrated. We don't realize that we have come under the control of the *Judge* and its ploys to distract and frustrate us. It is a very subtle process, but it has a profound effect on our lives.

The concept of the *Judge* is useful in understanding some critical psychological processes related to relationships within many families, organizations and various cultural institutions. When *Judge*-dominated individuals are in a position of power and control, they tend to use the organization's rules and regulations to control and manipulate their subordinates, associates and clients of the organization. At times when economic and social conditions deteriorate, there is a strong tendency for the *Judge* in different individuals to gain ascendance. This leads to increased tension, anxiety and insecurity. We are likely to feel our *Judge* more intensely when external conditions become unpredictable, unstable and more insecure. Communication tends to take place from a *Judge*-dominated perspective which distracts and confuses others. This type of *Judge*-dominated communication often leads to a takeover of institutions and organizations by the *Judge* part of the personality within key individuals and administrators. That is, the *Judge* part of an individual's personality becomes ever more dominant, usually without his or her awareness of this psychological process.

Stress is dramatically increased as *Judge*-domination occurs. Individuals are more likely to feel their own *Judge* because it triggers stress and tension in the body. Thus, a vicious cycle associated with stress begins and builds momentum. In *Judge*-dominated organizations and institutions, including families, not only is there a high level of stress and tension, but there is also distraction and difficulty with concentration. The verbal messages and expectations of the *Judge* are either internalized, leading to self-criticism, self-blame, depression, despair and self-destruction or externalized, leading to scapegoating, blaming others and aggressive hostile acting out. With the *Judge* concept, we can develop treatment techniques to more effectively shrink this destructive and lethal component in personality.

The *Judge* and the Rate of Social Change

Whenever there is substantial change in people's lives, there is fertile ground for the *Judge* to emerge and to take psychological control. This is a basic principle whether the change is in an individual's life or whether the change involves large portions of society. Today, we live under social and economic conditions that change incredibly fast and the rate of change is increasing all the time. Very few people can anticipate and adapt to the pace and direction of these changes. All of us are caught up in these changes which bring on intense stress, because we sense that we have no control over what is happening to us and to those around us. Still, some people, a fortunate few, actually thrive in these rapidly changing times. They have vision and are able to see opportunities arising out of the uncertainty of rapid change, whereas most of us perceive that whatever security and stability we do have is seriously threatened by these very same changes. The lucky few retain their sense of control and seem to be able to keep their *Judge* at bay. They don't become distracted and discouraged by its threats and manipulations. They can remain calm and cool, focused and confident in themselves and their abilities. They don't get caught up in self-doubt and lose confidence and hope. They are able to function in a relatively *Judge*-free manner.

Judge-Domination of Our Health Care System

We also see similar trends in the health care field. As we observed above, there are ample opportunities for the *Judge* to take over and dominate our healthcare delivery system. This happens most commonly when finances and cost concerns become critical issues. Controlling costs has become the dominant issue in health care today as "managed" health care affects the lives of more people. This is truly fertile ground for the *Judge* to take over and dominate the delivery of health care services in America today. In our view, this is an extremely **unhealthy** development because the *Judge* is, by its very nature, an **anti-life** force and psychological entity. It is inherently unhealthy.

When the *Judge* dominates the delivery of both mental and physical health care services, it will tend to destroy the very best of health care practices. Excellence will be replaced with mediocrity or worse. Finance and cost factors, not clinical expertise and knowledge, will drive healthcare decisions to meet the healthcare needs of individuals. Dr. Norman Shealy in his book *Third Party Rape* describes this process in great detail. In Dr. Shealy's view, there is constant interference with the doctor-patient relationship, often accompanied by long delays in obtaining essential treatment. Dr. Shealy expresses deep concern about greed, bureaucracy and power politics shaping the delivery of our health care services. The *Judge* is the driving psychological force which fuels this highly dysfunctional system in the same way that the *Judge* fuels alcoholism, drug addiction and codependence. The longer the *Judge* dominates our health care services, the more damage will be done to the delivery of quality health care. This often puts people's lives at greater risk. For example, a TV news item in February 1996 described how laboratory technicians, pressured to view too many Pap smears for economic efficiency, were making increasing numbers of errors, sometimes with tragic or fatal outcomes.

At some point in the not too distant future, we will have reached a point of "no return" in the destruction of quality health care. The *Judge,* operating in a managed care environment, can do irreparable damage to the entire system of health care services. Under such a dysfunctional system, the *Judge* creates rigid dogma in regard to health care concepts and treatments. Under managed care, all too frequently, the *Judge* makes the crucial clinical decisions. This does not bode well for the delivery of quality health care services. Freedom of choice in health care is the first casualty of such a system.

Economic Pressures and the *Judge*

Because of economic pressures and uncertainties, most of our organizations and institutions remain *Judge*-dominated or are becoming more so. Under these conditions, many of these organizations and institutions are strongly attracted to other *Judge*-dominated systems such as managed health care. They speak the same language and use the same ploys to manipulate and control people. Advertising and press releases use words to create the illusion of substance and quality in health care. It is not unusual today to hear a news report of a tragic error in a patient's treatment at a particular hospital and during the same day, we may hear an enticing radio or TV advertisement for that same hospital and its wonderful health care.

Many people working in *Judge*-dominated systems will become more insecure and anxious, feeling even more intense stress when confronted by rapid social and economic change. *Judge*-domination will lead to a significant drop in morale because people will feel less and less control over their own lives and even less control in their workplace. With *Judge*-domination, power and control issues take over the day-to-day lives of many people. Their ability to cope with stress diminishes with each successive round of rapid social and economic change. As their stress increases, people will have much more difficulty with their relationships at home and at work. Marriages will be severely tested and family life will suffer.

As we have seen, the *Judge* is frequently active in most workplaces. Nearly all of us have experienced the *Judge* operating in our places of work. The very nature of businesses or other enterprises which involve buying and selling of goods and services, cash flow, profit and loss and the control of costs of operation provide fertile ground for the *Judge* to operate. Evaluating a person's job performance is very difficult to do without the *Judge* taking over the process. Nevertheless, let's look and see how the process might work.

How can you tell if the *Judge* is manifest in your workplace? Is there chaos? Do schedules and priorities seem to change without apparent reason, keeping people off balance, increasing stress, interfering with productivity and, ultimately, morale? Does it feel like someone has sapped the life energy out of the place? Is creativity stifled or even dead?

Today's workers are faced with more and more problems to solve with fewer resources and in less time. Either wittingly or unwittingly, the *Judge* has really taken over the running of our businesses and industries. When this happens, quality and service are bound to suffer. There are constant pressure and tension with no tolerance for error or failure. The *Judge* demands perfection no matter what the human cost in terms of excess stress and "burnout." Power and control issues are taken to the extreme so that workers become demoralized and, after awhile, perform even more poorly. Work becomes total drudgery. When this happens, it is devastating to the human spirit.

A *Judge*-Free Workplace

The great challenge for most people is whether they can change their work environment into a more *Judge*-free one. A *Judge*-free work environment is vital to creative problem solving and avoiding burnout from excessive stress. How can you recognize a *Judge*-free work environment? In such an environment, life and energy abound. Creativity flourishes. People look forward to coming to work. People do their best work. They feel that management values and appreciates their efforts. Information is shared between workers and management, built on trust, respect and motivation. When schedules and priorities change, there is a clear understanding of why changes are necessary and everyone pulls together to get the job done. There is a big difference between internal motivation — "I can see that this is really important and I'm going to do my share to make it happen" vs. external motivation — "Do it because I say so!" Starhawk, in her book *Truth or Dare,* calls this "Power-with" vs. "Power-over."

Finally, in a *Judge*-free workplace, there is respect for individual differences. For example, flextime allows employees to start their workday anytime between 6:00 a.m. and 9:00 a.m. and finish between 3:00 p.m. and 6:00 p.m.. People can work during their own peak periods of productivity, avoid traffic hassles, arrange day care, etc. This flexibility enables people to effectively juggle their responsibilities to work, family and community.

Coping with Rapid Change

All too often, the intense stress triggered by social and economic change inflates the *Judge,* adding to the stress we already feel. Many of us become depressed or highly anxious as our *Judge* becomes more dominant under these changing conditions. A vicious cycle has been created involving the rate of social and economic change, increased stress that inflates the psychological power of the *Judge*, stress-related psychological and medical conditions and diminished ability to adapt to further social and economic change. For many people, the faster the rate of change, the more intense their stress becomes, the more the *Judge* dominates, and then, our coping reactions deteriorate.

Unfortunately, there is very little that most people can do to slow the rate of social and economic change. However, we believe that you can do a great deal to reduce the adverse impact of these changes on your life. In time, you can probably reverse your perception of this process of rapid change. You may learn to confront each new round of change from a position of psychological strength (*Warrior* energy) and confidence in your abilities rather than from a position of weakness and fear (*inner wounded child*).

One of the most effective ways to accomplish this is to recognize and understand the role of the *Judge* within ourselves, our families and the organizations that are major parts of our society. Taking steps to reduce the power of the *Judge* over our own lives will help us cope much better with the rate of change in our society. When you deal with the *Judge*, you break the vicious cycle involving social and economic change, stress and the *Judge*. As you confront and defuse your *Judge*, the nature of this vicious cycle will be substantially altered for you. You will become strengthened and empowered to deal more confidently with the next cycle of economic and social change. These external changes may be out of your personal control, but you will be able to better control your own <u>internal</u> response to the stress of change. As you become more psychologically empowered and self-confident, you will no longer need to feel threatened by change. Instead, you will be able to more effectively adapt to the constantly changing social and economic environment, dealing more successfully with the challenges as you encounter them. This will happen because your *inner child* will no longer be so easily overwhelmed by your *Judge* taking control as your stress increases.

Some psychologists talk about conditions which produce a "flow" experience which results when an external challenge is in congruence with your own internal abilities. Such conditions produce a natural "high" and enable you to deal effectively and successfully with any challenge which arises. A flow experience is very satisfying because you are in harmony with your environment. You have confidence in yourself and focus on the task in which you are involved. You have a strong intrinsic motivation to be involved in the activity. An active uncontrolled *Judge* will be a major inhibitor to flow because the *Judge* distracts you and blocks your response. The *Judge* diminishes your ability and strength to focus on the task at hand, making it much more difficult to handle. The *Judge* exploits and dominates the natural chaotic organization of the mind. This results in focusing your thinking on negative thoughts. In order achieve a situation of flow, the *Judge* must be dormant and under control in your psychological functioning. To experience flow, shrinking your *Judge* is essential.

A *Judge*-Free Environment

The more we become aware of the *Judge* and the stress that it brings on, the more we recognize its presence in common everyday situations. Some people intuitively have sensed the presence of the *Judge* in their place of work or school or even in their family. At a certain point of stress, they decide that it is just not worth the price they pay emotionally or physically to continue to expose themselves to such conditions. They quit their job or they leave school or they move away from their family. For some people, it literally becomes a life or death decision. They intuitively sense that the intense stress will make them sick or even kill them if they don't get out. They are willing to take a cut in pay or to make some other sacrifice in order to reduce the unbearable stress. Some people can do this without being fully aware that it is the *Judge* that they have chosen to leave.

Still, as more and more people become aware of the *Judge* in different places in their lives, they will be able to make a clearer connection between the *Judge* and the intense stress that they experience every day. As they develop this awareness, many will notice that they have less and less tolerance for the intense stress brought on by the *Judge* in the workplace, in school, in the family or in close relationships.

With this increased awareness, some will want to seek what we call a *Judge*-free environment. There are many features or characteristics of such an environment. It is generally calm and it feels safe. There is caring, warmth and understanding, or when needed, appropriate nurturing and healing are available. People feel supported and encouraged in an atmosphere of aliveness. Spirituality and creativity thrive under such *Judge*-free conditions and there is a balance of cooperation and shared responsibility. There is also clear communication between people and clear reasonable expectations exist.

Our close friend and colleague, Ann Scanlan, has a saying that she often uses in her therapy work: "You cannot not know what you now know." Once you are aware of the *Judge* and know how it operates, blocking aliveness, spirituality or creativity, you cannot not know its threatening vibe and destructive impact in people's lives. This awareness brings us to a crucial choice point. Do we really want to make positive changes in our lives and create life enhancing conditions within ourselves and those around us? Choosing to confront and to shrink our *Judge* requires courage and determination (*Warrior* energy).

We believe that the concept of the *Judge* and its relationship to the *inner child* and the *Warrior* archetype in the psychological model that we have described in this book gives us all some powerful psychological tools. We can effectively apply them to make profound changes in our own individual lives and in our society. Our vision is that we are all capable of creating a healthier, more *Judge*-free environment. This is our hope for our children and our grandchildren. That would be the best legacy we could leave for them.

ꓱFERENCES AND SUGGESTED READINGS

The Awakened Warrior. Rick Fields, Ed. G.P. Putnam, New York, NY, 1994.

Awakening in Time: The Journey from Codependence to Co-Creation. Small, Jacqueline. Bantam Books, New York, NY, 1991.

Beyond Therapy, Beyond Science: A New Model for Healing the Whole Person. Schaef, Anne Wilson. Harper & Row, New York, NY, 1992.

The Celestine Prophesy. Redfield, James, 1993.

Chaos: Making a New Science. Gleick, James, Penguin, 1988.

Companies with a Conscience: Intimate Portraits of Twelve Firms that Make a Difference. Scott, Mary & Howard Rothman, 1992.

Embracing Your Inner Critic: Turning Self-Criticism into a Creative Asset. Stone, Hal & Sidra. Harper Collins, New York, NY, 1993.

The Female Advantage: Women's Ways of Leadership. Helgesen, Sally. Doubleday, New York, NY, 1990.

Flight of the Buffalo: Soaring to Excellence, Learning to Let Employees Lead. Belasco, James A., & Ralph C. Stayer. Warner Books, New York, NY, 1993.

Healing the Child Within. Whitfield, Charles L., M.D. Health Communications, Deerfield Beach, FL, 1987.

Healing the Shame That Binds You. Bradshaw, John, Health Communications, FL, 1989.

Homecoming: Reclaiming and Championing Your Inner Child. Bradshaw, John. Bantam Books, New York, NY, 1990.

Humanistic Psychotherapy: The Rational Emotive Approach. Ellis, Albert. McGraw-Hill, 1974.

Joy's Way: A Map for the Transformational Journey: An Introduction to the Potentials for Healing with Body Energies. Joy, Brugh, M.D. Jeremy P. Tarcher, Los Angeles, CA, 1990.

King, Warrior, Magician, Lover. Moore, Robert & Doug Gillette. Harper, San Francisco, CA, 1990.

Love, Medicine and Miracles. Seigel, Bernie S., M.D. Harper & Row, New York, NY, 1986.

Magic, Science, and Religion and Other Essays. Malinowski, Bronislaw. Doubleday, Garden City, NY, 1948.

Minding the Body, Mending the Mind. Borysenko, Joan, Ph.D. Bantam Books, New York, NY, 1987.

One Emotion. Black, Clint. CD. "Wherever You Go," Blackened Music, 1994.

The Passion of the Western Mind: Understanding the Ideas That Have Shaped Our World View. Tarnas, Richard. Ballantine Books, New York, NY, 1991.

A Primer of Freudian Psychology. Hall, Calvin. Mentor Books, New York, NY, 1954.

The Psychoanalytic Theory of Neurosis. Fenichel, Otto, M.D. W.W. Norton & Co., New York, NY, 1945.

Psychotherapy East and West: A Unifying Paradigm. Swami Ajaya, Ph.D. The Himalayan International Institute of Yoga Science and Philosophy, Honesdale, PA, 1983.

Reclaiming Our Health: Exploding the Medical Myth and Embracing the Source of True Healing. Robbins, John. H. J. Kraemer, Tiburon, CA, 1996.

Reclaiming the Inner Child. Jeremiah Abrams, Ed. Jeremy P. Tarcher, Inc., Los Angeles, CA, 1990.

Safe at Last: A Handbook for Recovery from Abuse. Schopick, David J., M.D. Waterfront Books, Burlington, VT, 1995.

Scripts People Live. Steiner, Claude. Bantam Books, New York, NY, 1974.

Third Party Rape. Shealy, Norman, M.D., Ph.D., Golde Press, MN, 1993.

Truth or Dare: Encounters with Power, Authority and Mystery. Starhawk. Harper & Row, San Francisco, 1987.

When Society Becomes an Addict. Schaef, Anne Wilson. Harper & Row, San Francisco, 1987.

Yoga and Psychotherapy: The Evolution of Consciousness. Swami Rama, Rudolph Ballentine, M.D., & Swami Ajaya, Ph.D. The Himalayan International Institute of Yoga Science and Philosophy, Honesdale, PA, 1976.

TO ORDER Rick and Rosalie Malter's books, audio and video cassette tapes on the *Judge*,

call:

1-800-882-3015

INFORMATION/REGISTRATION for 1 and 2 day *WORKSHOPS*, or 1 and 2 hour *SEMINARS*,

CALL:

1-800-882-3015

or write to:

The Malter Institute for Natural Development
2500 W. Higgins Road, Suite 355
Hoffman Estates, Illinois 60195
e-mail: RickMIND@aol.com

Please send a stamped, self addressed envelope.

****NOW AVAILABLE****

ADDITIONAL TOPICS ON AUDIO CASSETTE:

Stress and the *Judge*

The *Judge*, Money and Financial Security

The *Judge* and Relationships

The *Judge* in Addiction Recovery

The *Judge* In Sports

The *Judge* and Health Care

The *Judge* and Education

The *Judge* and Business

TO ORDER INFORMATION and ARTICLES on

Tissue Mineral Analysis:
Stress and the Mind/Body Connection

The Calcium "Shell"

Slow and Fast Metabolizers

Call

1-800-882-3015